INSIGHT POCKET GUIDE

GW00372371

PR

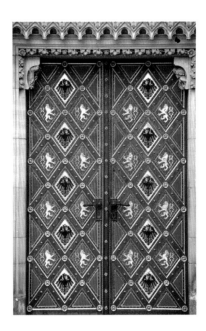

 PUBLICATIONS

Part of the Langenscheidt Publishing Group

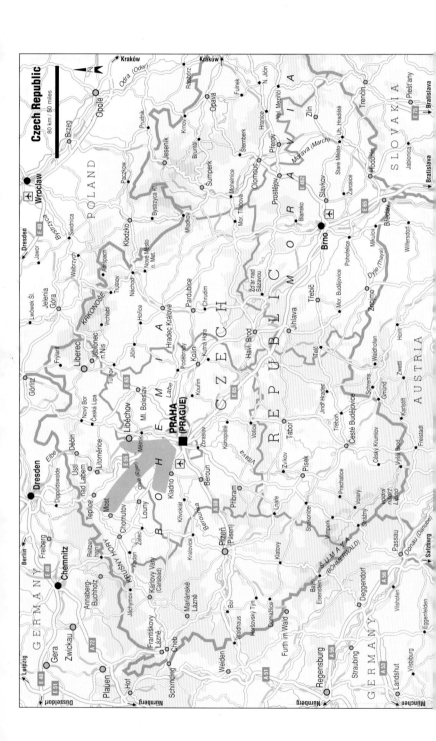

Welcome

This guidebook combines the interests and enthusiasms of two of the world's best-known information providers: Insight Guides, who have set the standard for visual travel guides since 1970, and Discovery Channel, the world's premier source of non-fiction television programming. Its purpose is to bring you the best of Prague and its surroundings in a series of tailor-made itineraries devised by Insight's correspondent in Prague, Alfred Horn. Prague is sometimes called the Golden City, and if you stand on the Charles Bridge, with the castle towering above and the sunlight glistening on the waters of the Vltava, you will understand why. The book explores this beautiful city in the course of 13 day or half-day itineraries, and suggests six excursions to places outside Prague, such as the spa town of Karlovy Vary (Carlsbad) and the brewing centre of Plzeň, offering something for all tastes.

Supporting the itineraries are sections on history and culture, shopping, eating out and nightlife, plus a fact-packed practical information section detailing everything from getting around the city to money matters and communications. This section includes a list of hand-picked hotels.

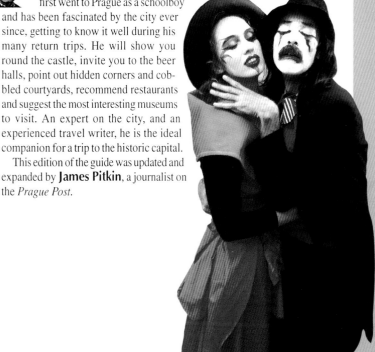

Alfred Horn is your guide to the Golden City. He is a German journalist who has edited a number of previous Insight Guides to eastern European destinations. He first went to Prague as a schoolboy and has been fascinated by the city ever since, getting to know it well during his many return trips. He will show you round the castle, invite you to the beer halls, point out hidden corners and cobbled courtyards, recommend restaurants and suggest the most interesting museums to visit. An expert on the city, and an experienced travel writer, he is the ideal companion for a trip to the historic capital.

This edition of the guide was updated and expanded by **James Pitkin**, a journalist on the *Prague Post*.

Pages 2/3: view from Charles Bridge towards the Old Town
Pages 8/9: the Fred and Ginger Building, the New Town

History & *Culture*

Every romantic city has a legend about its origins. In Prague's case the myth has been handed down by the chronicler Cosmas, who tells of the beautiful, brilliant Libuše. Under Libuše's guidance, her beloved husband Přemysl the farmer gave up tilling the soil and founded a city on the River Vltava 'in which, one day, two olive trees will grow up to the seventh heaven, and shine throughout the world with portents and wonder'.

By the 9th century, their descendants, the Přemyslids, had emerged as the dominant force among the family clans – they ruled great sections of Bohemia and Moravia from their castle, Praha, on the left bank of the Vltava. A hundred years later, the erection of Vyšehrad in the south and Hradčany on the heights opposite established the borders of today's city centre. Bohemia was part of the German empire and Prague, which consequently had access to Western Europe, became an important focal point for international trade.

The Přemyslid princes of Prague renovated and reinforced their fortress, and expanded St Vitus' Cathedral. They also founded Strahov Monastery outside the walls of Hradčany, and the monastery of the Knights of St John in the Lesser Town. At the foot of the castle hill, they established a new town, later called Malá Strana, for the Germans who had migrated to the country. On the opposite river bank, in the area of today's Old Town Square, Czech merchants and craftsmen embarked on an intense building programme. Thus did today's Old Town ('Staré Město') originate as a separate town. Malá Strana and 'Staré Město', both flourishing centres of trade, were rivals whose mutual antipathy was fuelled by a marked difference in their cultures.

The death of the last Přemyslid in 1305, and the subsequent struggles for power among foreign candidates for the throne, including Bohemian aristocrats and Prague patricians alike, led to a wave of destruction and plundering. In 1310, the nobles and clergymen elected the emperor's son, John of Luxembourg, as their king. Alas the new king had no interest in Prague and the city began a steady decline into a provincial backwater.

Charles IV's Golden Age

The city's fortunes only changed for the better with the arrival of the Duke of Luxembourg's son – who was to become Charles IV. It was under Charles's rule that Prague embarked on a Golden Age, whose influence can still be felt in the city today.

Born in Prague, Charles was raised in the court of his uncle, the King of France. At the age of 17 he returned to Prague as his father's regent, whereupon he industriously set about expanding the city of his childhood. His election as German king in 1349, and his subsequent coronation as Holy Roman Emperor in Rome in 1355,

Left: the city in 1493
Right: statue on the tomb of Ottokar I in St Vitus' Cathedral

conferred upon Prague the status of Imperial Residence. The town blossomed into a metropolis, and became a major political and cultural centre. Charles initiated a number of ambitious architectural projects, such as St Vitus' Cathedral and the Charles Bridge, which remain among the city's most memorable landmarks. He also established the New Town (Nové Město), thereby considerably expanding the municipal boundaries. One of the few highly educated rulers in the Europe of the Middle Ages, he attracted the finest minds of the time, and founded the first university in Central Europe. Charles University remains the nation's most prestigious academy to this day. Charles died in 1378, and was succeeded by his son, Wenceslas IV.

A Tradition of Defenestration

As the 14th century drew to a close, the Czech pastor Jan Hus began to preach against the secularisation of the church. He was supported by the common folk, by the citizens of Prague, and even by the king, so what had started as a theological dispute evolved into a widespread social and national movement. The clergy, backed by the nobility, imprisoned Hus and his followers. In 1415, despite assurances to the contrary, the Council of Constance condemned Hus to be burned at the stake. The sentence provoked a storm of protest in Prague and throughout Bohemia. In 1419 a mob stormed the New Town Hall, demanding the release of jailed Hussites. When their demands were not met, they threw several officials from the windows, establishing a tradition of Prague defenestrations.

The Hussites took over the city. They elected their own officials, and a Hussite army led by the military genius Jan Žižka liberated Bohemia, repeatedly trouncing imperial armies. But the movement was split by factions; the

Above: Jan Huss on his way to the pyre in Constance
Right: Charles IV – an educated monarch in medieval Europe

'Utraquists', supported by the Czech nobility and the wealthy middle classes, made peace with the Catholics and the empire. In 1458, George of Poděbrady, a Czech Utraquist, was crowned king of Bohemia. Having been destroyed and reduced to an economic shambles, Prague experienced a second flowering.

Enter the Habsburgs

Dreams of freedom and political autonomy were, however, realised for only two generations. In a portentous royal election, the Bohemians voted, against all historical logic, for Archduke Ferdinand I, a Catholic Habsburg. The new king sent soldiers to plunder the city, removed the privileges won by the Hussite Revolution, and restored the Church to its position of power.

A new era dawned when Rudolf II, who reigned from 1576 to 1612, moved the Habsburg residence to Prague. A true Renaissance ruler, Rudolf did much to enrich the city's artistic and architectural heritage, but at the expense of practical affairs, in which he had little interest. Rudolf II eventually had to concede the Bohemian crown to his brother. Prague's citizens took advantage of the royal family's internal squabble, winning a number of concessions regarding their rights. Meanwhile the fundamental conflict between foreign Catholic rulers and nationalist Hussites remained unresolved.

On 23 May 1618, three more city officials were thrown out of the castle windows – 'according to an old Czech tradition', as a voice cried from the angry crowd – and the powder keg exploded. The Thirty Years' War began, and Bohemia and its flourishing metropolis drew the short straw. In November 1620 the united armies of the emperor and the Catholic League marched into the city and Prague's dreams of being a world power were at an end. For three centuries, the Habsburgs governed all of Central Europe from Vienna; Prague had to be satisfied with the role of provincial capital. At least a few generously appointed palaces were built, such as that of Count Albrecht von Wallenstein.

After the pan-European revolutionary upheavals of 1848, the Czech nationalist movement centred on Prague. In 1861, a Czech was elected mayor for the first time; 20 years later the National Theatre, built with public donations, opened with a gala performance of Smetana's *Libuše*.

The 20th Century

Czechoslovakia was proclaimed a republic in 1918 at the end of World War I. There was much jubilation in Prague's streets at the return of Tomáš Garrigue Masaryk and Edvard Beneš from exile. Both men would later serve as the country's president. Prague became a lively capital city once again as the result of an agreement reached with the Slovaks about the formation of a union. In the interwar years the new nation benefited from a thriving economy and an arts scene that recognised the importance of the relatively new film industry.

Right: Count Albrecht von Wallenstein, remembered for his palace

The Munich Pact of 1938 ceded the Sudetenland to Hitler, thereby sealing the fate of the First Republic. Not satisfied with the large swathes of border territory that it acquired from the pact, Nazi Germany invaded Prague on 15 March 1939. The Nazis established the Protectorate of Bohemia and Moravia, and Slovakia became a fascist puppet state. As the Nazis retreated from Prague at the end of World War II, they maliciously burnt down the north wing of the Old Town Hall. The Czech people welcomed the Soviet Union's Red Army into the city, and the communists took over the reins of government in 1948 with very little effort. But before long Stalinist terror, and the Communist Party's compliance, destroyed all Czech hopes of finding a path to the spirit of socialism.

The Prague Spring

The Prague Spring – as the tumultuous events of 1968 became known – was rooted in the near collapse of the country's economy. In that year the reformer Alexander Dubček became an internationally feted figure due to his programme of reform, entitled 'Socialism with a human face'. A ground swell of support for Dubček, with writers, dramatists, artists and intellectuals playing a leading role, became impossible to ignore. Dubček's programme, had it been realised, would have laid the foundations for a more free and equitable society. Its details included federal autonomy for the Slovaks, long overdue industrial and agricultural reforms, and a revised constitution that would guarantee civil rights and liberties and democratisation of the country and party. Not for the first time, the dreams of Prague's citizenry were crushed by a foreign army: the Soviet Union marched in with soldiers from five Warsaw Pact countries on 21 August 1968.

But the spark lit in Prague continued to glow. Scarcely a decade later, a group of intellectuals formed the human-rights group Charter 77. The co-founder, the poet and playwright Václav Havel, went on to lead the Velvet

Revolution. As the Iron Curtain, behind which the peoples of Eastern Europe had been incarcerated since the end of World War II, began to disintegrate, the people of Prague elected the persecuted dissident Havel president in November 1989. They were heady days. But, after decades of totalitarian Soviet control, the country could not be expected to make the transition to democracy and a market economy overnight. The problems, such as widespread economic corruption, and the process of coming to terms with the years of Soviet oppression, were enormous. Moreover, the differences between Czechs and Slovaks were becoming increasingly bitter.

On 1 January 1993, Czechs and Slovaks formed their own separate republics. Havel resigned over the 'Velvet Divorce', only to return a month later as Czech president. Miloš Zeman became prime minister of a minority Social Democrat government kept in power by an agreement with the right-wing opposition Civic Democratic Party. In 1995 the Czech Republic became the first post-communist state to join the Organisation for Economic Cooperation and Development, an important step on the road to the long-term goal of full membership in the European Union. The country joined NATO in 1999, along with Hungary and Poland. The years since the Velvet Divorce have not been easy, but the people of Prague retain their optimism and sense of humour. They are coping well with the social turbulence around them, and the city has emerged as a centre for international tourists.

Culture in the Czech Capital

Prague is home to more than three dozen theatres, three opera houses, some two dozen museums, and a growing number of galleries. In this creative city every day sees the ripening of new ideas, and the realisation of frequently radical concepts and projects in the arts. Throughout centuries of oppression by foreign rulers, the people of Prague supported literature, music and the visual arts as the means to preserve and express their national identity.

The composer Bedřich Smetana (1824–84), renowned in Prague during his lifetime, was one of the most determined of Czech nationalists. His symphonic poem *Má Vlast* (My Fatherland), and his opera *Libuše*, both gave expression to the national cultural iden-

tity. Since 1946, the famous 'Prague Spring' music festival has always commenced on 12 May, the date of Smetana's death, and *Má Vlast* is always played at the opening concert.

The popularity of music in Prague, both private and public, was remarked upon as early as 1772 by the English musicologist Charles Burney, who claimed that the Czechs were 'the most musical people of Europe'. Throughout the year, untold numbers of Prague citizens play recitals, be it in private apartments or fine palaces and churches. And, although rock, pop and jazz have

Above Left: Hitler invades Czechoslovakia. **Left:** memorial to the Prague Spring
Above and Following Page: Prague is an international centre for many art forms

established their presence, classical music continues to play a significant role in the country's cultural life.

Literature has also served as an influential force on Prague's cultural scene. Jaroslav Hašek and Franz Kafka, representatives of an epoch of literary history, used satire and parable to express themselves without interference from the censors. Kafka in particular has won a reputation as one of the greatest writers of the 20th century. Their successors under communist dictatorship also faced censorship, particularly after 1968, when there was a serious threat of blacklisting or imprisonment. Some of the finest of the current generation of writers, such as Milan Kundera and Josef Skvorecký, went into exile, while those who stayed, such as Ivan Klíma and Václav Havel, suffered the consequences: their works were banned and they were imprisoned or forced to do the most menial of jobs.

The Czechoslovak New Wave

The creative energy of the Czechs and the Slovaks has been particularly evident in cinema. In the 1960s Miloš Forman and Jiří Menzel attracted international interest in a movement that became known as the Czechoslovak New Wave. Prague's Barrandov Studios, the largest in Europe, have attracted Hollywood blockbuster projects and in recent years a new generation of Czech film-makers has emerged. One of the most eminent of the new crop of directors is Jan Svěrák, whose 1995 *Kolja* won an Oscar for best foreign film.

The spectacular Laterna Magika company, which rose to international prominence at the World Exhibition in Brussels in 1958, presents its Black Light shows, a synthesis of film, pantomime and acting, at the Nová Scéna (which is now itself known as the Laterna Magika). Next door to this building, the splendid National Theatre – which stages opera as well as drama – has long been a symbol of national pride and the leading venue for artists and performers who spearhead an independent cultural movement.

In Prague, political developments are often led by art and culture, rather than the other way round. Artists treasure their acknowledged responsibility towards society, and often act as spokesmen for their fellow citizens. Most citizens are passionate in their identification with their artists: they discuss them, criticise them, and love them fervently. There are few places where art and culture play such an important role in the everyday life of ordinary citizens.

HISTORY HIGHLIGHTS

25,000 BC A highly developed Stone Age culture moves into Southern Moravia, leaving the legacy of the Venus of Věstonice, the oldest unearthed ceramic in the world.

c 1,000 BC Celts settle on the Vltava.

1st century BC German tribes settle and hold their own in battles against the Roman Empire.

6th century AD Slavic tribes drive out the Germans and settle the region.

623–4 The Frankish merchant and war hero Samo is crowned king, and his Slavic army drives out Frankish invaders. Samo's empire dissolves after his death.

9th century The Sixth Empire is formed. According to legend, Přemysl and Libuše founded the new Czech dynasty.

907 Invading Hungarians take over Slovakia, which remains in their possession until 1918.

1029 Under Václav (Wenceslas I, the Holy) the country becomes Christian, preparing the way for unification of Bohemia and Moravia.

1212 With the Golden Bull of Bohemia, Emperor Friedrich II turns the unified territory into a hereditary kingdom.

1306 End of the Přemyslid dynasty.

1316 Charles IV is born in Prague.

1333 Charles IV's father gives him responsibility for Bohemia and Moravia.

1348 The first university in Central Europe opens in Prague.

1355 Pope Innocent VI crowns Charles IV emperor in Rome. Prague becomes the capital.

c 1400 Charles's son Wenceslas IV is criticised by the Czech pastor Jan Hus, who also attacks the church for its drift towards secularisation.

1415 Hus is burned as a heretic.

1419 Revolt against the German upper class. Hussites demand a Czech national state.

1458 George of Poděbrady is the last ruler of Czech nationality prior to the 20th century.

1526 The Bohemians elect the Habsburg Ferdinand king.

1583 Rudolf II moves his residence from Vienna to Hradčany.

1618 Angry citizens throw imperial administrators from the palace windows, thereby sparking the Thirty Years' War.

1620 Beginning of era of Habsburg rule, which lasts until 1918.

1918 The Czechoslovak Republic is proclaimed. Tomáš Garrigue Masaryk is elected first president.

1938 Munich Pact. Hitler uses the alleged discrimination against the German minority in Czechoslovakia as a pretext to invade in March 1939.

1945 Prague is liberated by the Soviet Red Army at end of World War II.

1948 In a free election, the Communists receive 38 percent of the vote. The country becomes the Socialist Republic of Czechoslovakia.

1968 Warsaw Pact tanks crush Dubček's 'Prague Spring'.

1977 Founding of the civil rights group Charter 77.

1989 The 'Velvet Revolution' introduces a free, federalist constitution to Czechoslovakia. Václav Havel is elected president.

1993 On 1 January the Czechs and Slovaks split into two republics.

1999 The Czech Republic joins NATO.

2000 There are violent anti-globalisation protests at the annual IMF/World Bank summit in Prague.

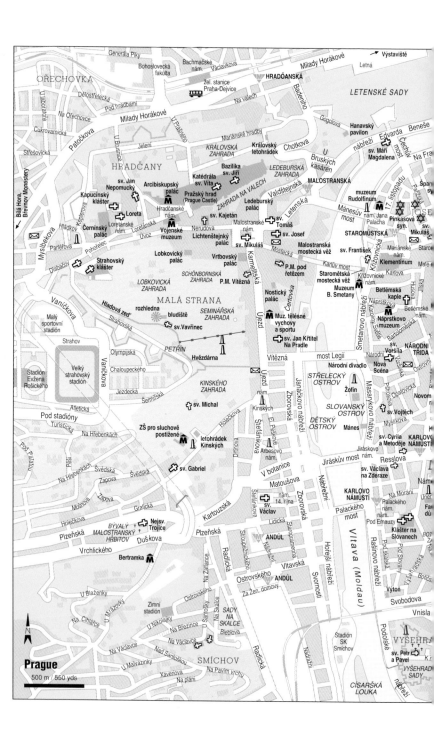

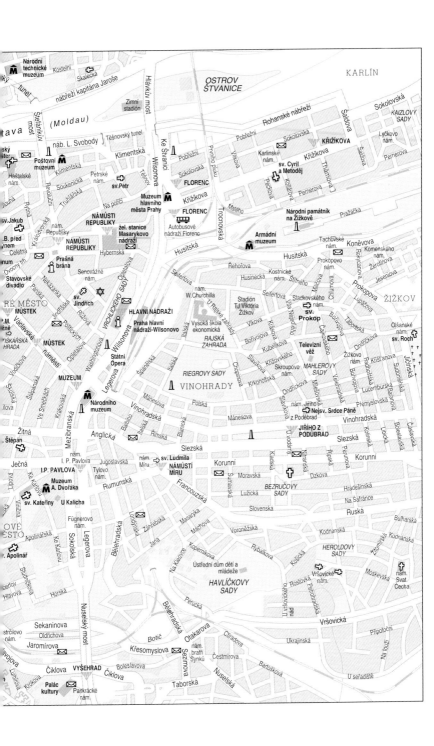

City Itineraries

1. THE OLD TOWN *(see map p22)*

A leisurely stroll through the winding streets of the Old Town. After enjoying the tranquillity of the Jewish cemetery, and the contrasting bustle of the Old Town Square, dine in style in the Hotel Paříž.

Wherever you are staying in Prague, begin this itinerary with a long breakfast in Wenceslas Square (Václavské náměstí).

Wenceslas Square – actually more of a broad boulevard – lies at the heart of the New Town. To the left and right, broad pedestrian zones follow the course of the fortifications that surrounded the city in the Middle Ages, before Charles IV erected the New Town in a semicircle around the old.

Take the small street **Na můstku** which, by way of Melantrichova, leads to the colourful features of the Old Town. After only a few paces, you will stumble on an **open-air market**, where stalls sell all manner of fresh produce, crafts, wooden toys and other souvenirs. Backtrack to Melantrichova, which will take you to the **Old Town Hall** (Staroměstská radnice), dating from the end of the 13th century. Here, take a brief look around the **Old Town Square** with its churches, palaces and splendid residences; the itinerary returns here in the afternoon. Particularly distinguished is the Town Hall's **Astronomical Clock** (Orloj) which, dating from 1410, preserves on its face the medieval view of the course of the sun and moon: the earth is located at the centre of the universe. At the very top of the clock, the figure of Death appears every hour to ring the bells and let the hour glass of life run out. The Apostles march past in two open windows above, then a cockerel crows before the clock strikes the hour.

Hus Preached Here

Beyond the Town Hall, which today has little other than a decorative function, is **Small Square** (Malé náměstí), where there's a fountain with a lovely Renaissance grille and a fancy-foods shop with an elaborately painted facade. Follow the bend in Karlova Street and you will see the Herculean figures on the **Clam-Gallas Palace** (Clam-Gallasův palác) on Husova Street to your right; this is a well-restored high-baroque house that now contains the city archives. Turn left into Husova Street and take the third street on the right to reach the **Bethlehem Chapel** (Betlémská kaple). Jan Hus delivered his fiery sermons against bigotry and ostentation in this simple house of worship. Next door, Hus's house has an exhibition of his life and work. On the west side of Betlémské náměstí square, the **Ethnological Museum** (Náprstkovo muzeum) surrounds a pretty courtyard and café.

Left: the Astronomical Clock presents a medieval world-view
Right: one of the clock's apostles, which emerges from a window

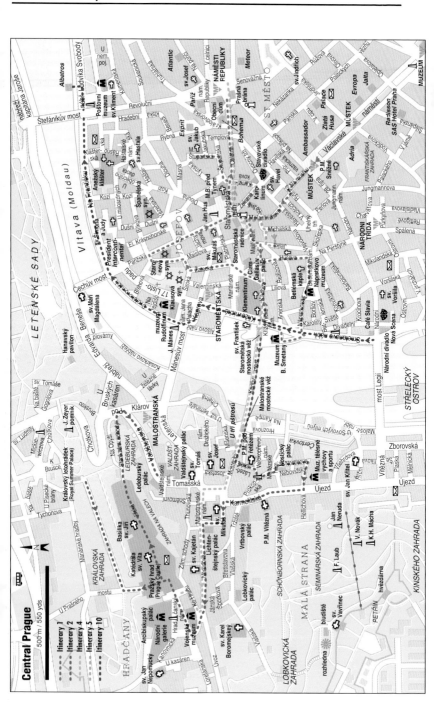

Náprstkova Street leads to the river. Here, beyond the embankment, a small terrace in front of the **Smetana Museum** (Muzeum Bedřicha Smetany, open daily Wed–Mon 10am–noon, 12.30–5pm) offers what is probably the most famous vantage point for photographers of the **Charles Bridge** (Karlův most) and **Hradčany** *(see Itinerary 2, page 25)*. Beyond the former mill-houses, at the start of the Charles Bridge, are the **Old Town Bridge Tower** and the **Church of St Francis of Assisi**, known as the Crusaders' Church, with its magnificently painted dome. Across the road is the baroque facade of **St Salvator**, which is part of the sprawling complex of the **Klementinum**. This college was founded by Jesuits summoned to the country in 1556 by the Habsburgs to spearhead the Counter-Reformation. Today, the Klementinum serves as the city library and as a concert venue.

The Jewish Quarter

At the end of this massive complex, Platnéřská Street on the right leads to Marianské nám. Just past the city library, turn left into Zatecká and you will find yourself in the **Jewish Quarter**. The sites of the former Jewish Town are accessed via the Široká Street entrance to the **Jewish Cemetery**. A ticket to the **Jewish Museum** (open daily 9am–5.30pm except Sat and Jewish holy days) is good for all of the quarter's sites except the Old-New Synagogue. At the grave of Rabbi Loew in the Jewish Cemetery, Jews honour the great teacher and creator of the *golem*, the clay monster that, it was believed, protected the inhabitants of the ghetto.

Not far from the exit point are both the **Klaus Synagogue**, which exhibits assorted artefacts of Jewish life, and the **Pinkas Synagogue**, known for its poignant collection of drawings by Jewish children in the Terezín concentration camp. On the corner of Maislova stands the **Old-New Synagogue** (open Sun–Thur 9am–6pm, Fri 9am–5pm) which, dating to the 1270s, is the oldest Jewish house of worship still in use in Europe. Its lovely brick gable shows clear traces of the strict order of Cistercian Gothic. Opposite is the **Jewish Town Hall**, originally built in the Renaissance style and only later embellished with baroque elements. Have a close look at the gable, in particular the clock, whose hands, in keeping with the Hebrew practice of reading from right to left, move in an anti-clockwise direction. For lunch in the Jewish Quarter, two recommended options are: **U Golema**, Maislova 8 (tel: 232 81 65), and **U Červeného kola** in Anežská Street, behind St Agnes' Cloister (tel: 24 81 11 18).

Above: motif in the Jewish quarter
Right: statue of the nationalist composer Smetana

After lunch, a last look around the quarter might take in the Art Nouveau facades that line Pařížská Street. Wander back down this stylish avenue to the Old Town Square, where you will see the ornate facade of **St Nicholas' Church**, built in the 1730s by Kilián Ignáz Dientzenhofer, to your right. The Old Town Square (Staroměstské náměstí) is the midpoint of the Old Town, and the heart of Prague. In the centre stands the **Jan Hus Monument**, erected on 6 July 1915, to commemorate the 500th anniversary of his death. The **Týn Church** that towers over the scene forms a breathtaking backdrop.

On the north side of the square **House No 7** was once a Pauline monastery; on the east side, the **Kinský Palace** presents a facade decidedly influenced by the rococo style. At the foot of the church towers, next to one another, are the Gothic **House at the Stone Bell**, the **Týn School**, and the **House at the White Unicorn**. The Týn School, a Gothic building rebuilt in the style of the Venetian Renaissance, and Celetná No 5 provide the two entrances to the **Týn Church**, noteworthy for its Bohemian baroque paintings and the oldest baptismal font in Prague.

A Unique Organ

Behind the church, from Štupartská, an alley called Malá Stupartská leads left to the **Church of St James**. Built by the Minorites in the reign of Charles IV, the church was renovated during the baroque period. You may have an opportunity to catch one of the many recitals given on the church's wonderfully decorated, uniquely toned organ, built in 1705 (check the poster by the door for times).

Trace your steps back to the Old Town Square and stroll down Celetná Street, the

Top: Týn Church in Old Town Square
Above: baroque reliefs, Church of St James

city itineraries

beginning leg of the Royal Way *(see page 35)*. On the corner of Ovocný trh stands the **House of the Black Madonna**. Constructed in 1912 – the first Cubist building in Prague – this was originally a department store, but now it houses a branch of the Czech Museum of Fine Art, and features a permanent exhibition of Cubist painting, sculpture and furniture.

At the end of Celetná is the mighty **Powder Tower** (Prašná brána). In 1475, on the very spot where a fortified tower protected the Old Town in the 13th century, King Jagiello had a new defensive structure erected, directly beside his royal court, but its importance diminished after the residence was moved to Hradčany. The tower's name derives from its use as a powder magazine in the 18th century. The building was renovated at the end of the 19th century, when a new roof was added; from the top, reached by a long spiral staircase, visitors can enjoy a lovely view over the Old Town.

Next door, on the site of the former Royal Court, is the Art Nouveau **Municipal House** (Obecní dům). The building and its Smetana Hall (a splendid concert venue), were recently renovated. You might stop for some late-afternoon refreshments in its street-level café or in the basement's baroque beer hall, which incorporates elegant Art Nouveau touches. Conclude your tour with dinner in the **Sarah Bernhardt restaurant** (tel: 236 08 20) in the renowned **Hotel Paříž** which, dating to 1907, is located behind the Municipal House. The restaurant's original Art Nouveau decor is complemented by Bohemian cuisine refined with a touch of French sophistication.

2. CHARLES BRIDGE, LESSER TOWN AND HRADČANY CASTLE *(see map p22)*

From the Old Town Bridge Tower cross Charles Bridge to the Lesser Town Square. Stroll up the elegant Nerudova to Hradčany Castle and to St Vitus' Cathedral. Dine on traditional Lesser Town fare.

Start early in the morning at the Old Town Bridge Tower (Staromětská mostecká věž). Take the metro to Staromětská station and turn left along the embankment.

In the morning mists, the city on either side of the Vltava resembles a stage set, blurred by a fog of make-believe. Behind you is the Old Town, the centre of bourgeois Prague, where knowledge and trade have flowered for centuries, giving rise to an international, cosmopolitan culture.

On the other side of the river, the city has another face. The **Lesser Town** (Malá Strana) used to be a neighbourhood of simple workers and fishermen living in the shadow of the rulers' residential city. The nobles' elaborate palaces, the monasteries, churches, and the imperial cathedral were crowded together on the heights of **Hradčany**. The whole city was dominated by a castle that served as the home of the ruling families for a millennium.

Right: statue of St Wenceslas

Charles Bridge

Charles IV hoped that **Charles Bridge** (Karlův most) would unite the two rival settlements on opposite riverbanks into a single city. The magnificent stone bridge, created by Peter Parler, constitutes the central section of the Royal Way *(see page 35)*. Lining the sides of the bridge, statues of saints, now mostly copies of the baroque originals, gaze upon the waters below. The scene brings to mind the evocative music of Smetana's *Vltava*. To the right of the bridge, the silhouette of Hradčany Castle, crowned by the spires of St Vitus' Cathedral, is etched against the sky.

On the Malá Strana side of the bridge, the **Lesser Town Bridge Tower** (Malostranské mostecké věž) awaits visitors. To the right, beneath the bridge, is a romantic inn, the **Three Ostriches Hotel** (U tři pštrosů, Dražického nám. 12; tel: 57 53 24 10), where Goethe once stayed. Its restaurant is expensive by Prague standards, but the quality of its food is exceptionally good; you will need to reserve a table to dine here.

Just past the city gate, turn left into **Lázeňská**, passing the former luxury hotels **Spa** (V Lázních) and the **Golden Unicorn** (U zlatého jednorožce). You will soon come to the oldest Lesser Town church, **St Mary-under-the-Chain** (Kostel Panny Marie pod řetězem) with its ponderous Romanesque-Gothic facade. On the neighbouring square, Velokopřevorské náměstí, the **Maltese Grand Prior's Palace** houses a fine collection of musical instruments. The palace's gardens border the island of **Kampa** (Na Kampě), which can be reached by means of a small bridge over **Devil's Stream** (Čertovka). This 'Little Venice' neighbourhood was a popular meeting place for the city's flower children in the 1960s.

Lesser Town Square

Leaving the island for mainland Malá Strana, walk through Maltese Square (Maltézské ám), with its **Nostitz Palace** (Nostický palác). On Karmelitská Street, the **Vrtba Palace** (Vrtbovský palác) at No 25 is worth a look, above all for its terraced gardens. Back on Mostecká (Bridge Street), turn left into

Above: Charles Bridge.
Right: Church of St Nicholas

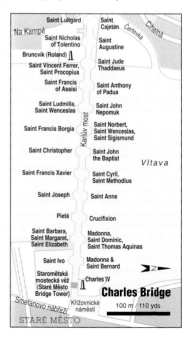

Na Kampě
Saint Luitgard
Saint Nicholas of Tolentino
Bruncvik (Roland)
Saint Vincent Ferrer, Saint Procopius
Saint Francis of Assisi
Saint Ludmilla, Saint Wenceslas
Saint Francis Borgia
Saint Christopher
Saint Francis Xavier
Saint Joseph
Pietá
Saint Barbara, Saint Margaret, Saint Elizabeth
Saint Ivo
Staroměstská mostecká věž (Staré Město Bridge Tower)

Saint Cajetan
Saint Augustine
Saint Jude Thaddaeus
Saint Anthony of Padua
Saint John Nepomuk
Saint Norbert, Saint Wenceslas, Saint Sigismund
Saint John the Baptist
Saint Cyril, Saint Methodius
Saint Anne
Crucifixion
Madonna, Saint Dominic, Saint Thomas Aquinas
Madonna & Saint Bernard
Charles IV

Čihelná
Čertovka
Karlův most
Vltava

Charles Bridge
100 m / 110 yds

Smetanovo nábřeží
Křižovnické náměstí
STARÉ MĚSTO

the **Lesser Town Square** (Malostranské nám), where the two towers of the mighty **Church of St Nicholas** (Kostel sv Mikuláše) rise towards the sky. Every detail of the church's interior, from its majestic ceiling murals to the pulpit and the ornately embellished chancel, reflects the absolutism that characterised the Counter Reformation Catholic Church. Contrast this with

the stark simplicity of Hus's Bethlehem Chapel *(see page 21)*. By this stage hunger pangs might well persuade you to part with these opulent surroundings.

Around the square there are characterful eateries in a number of hidden corners, courtyards, alleys and passageways. The top-class restaurant **U Mecenáš** (No 10; tel: 57 53 16 31) doesn't open until 5pm on weekdays (noon at weekends), and is a better bet for evening dining (reservations recommended), but you might want to check out the Renaissance building in which it is housed.

There's a far better chance of finding a seat at **U Schnellů** (Tomášská, No 6). New restaurants are opening all the time in the neighbourhood's picturesque back courtyards: explore this area at will and you are bound to be rewarded with a memorable meal. If you don't feel adventurous, there's always the café on the square. From here there are fine views of the **Town Hall** (No 21), which houses the **Obecní Galerie Beseda gallery** (open Tues–Sun 1–6pm), and of the **Montag House** (No 18, aka the Smiřický House), where the second and most significant Prague Defenestration was planned in 1618.

Nerudovna and the Castle

Should you be in need of some post-prandial exercise, climb the steep Nerudova road towards the castle. Formerly the main street to the castle, Nerudova is lined with dozens of mansions from virtually every architectural epoch. The imaginatively decorated facades, with house signs that once served as street addresses, help mark the route: a golden cup hangs from the **House at the Golden Goblet** (U zlaté číše, No 16), and three violins grace the **House of the Three Violins** (U tří housliček, No 34). Particularly worth seeing in Nerudova's lower section are the portal and a balcony held up by statues of Moors that adorn the **Morzin Palace** (Morzinský palác, No 5).

At the upper end, Nerudova narrows into a romantic stairway leading up to **Hradčanské nám**. To the left of the stairs, the Renaissance edifice of the former **Town Hall** is adorned with the imperial and state coats of arms. Here Loretánská leads off to the left towards the Loreto church and the formerly poverty-stricken neighbourhood of Nový Svět (New World): a separate itinerary is dedicated to this neighbourhood *(see Loreto and the 'New World', page 39)*.

Ceiling Murals

You should visit the **Schwarzenberg Palace** (daily except Mon, Fri, 10am–6pm), less for its military museum than for its impressive ceiling murals on the second floor. In theory you can also see the **Archbishop's Palace** (Arcibiskupský palác) if you are here on the Thursday before Easter (Maundy Thursday), but in recent years it has been closed for restoration.

More than 1,000 years old, **Hradčany Castle** (Pražský Hrad) was the residence of the early Přemyslid rulers, who did well to establish their headquarters in this strategic position over the Vltava. Generations of rulers continued to expand the complex with churches and palaces, defensive and residential buildings. Enter the castle through the first courtyard, and stand before the baroque **Mattias Gate** (Matyášova brána). To the right, a staircase leads up to the throne room, where the president hosts receptions for foreign diplomats. Of greater interest is the second courtyard, which has a lovely fountain and the **Chapel of the Holy Cross**, containing the church treasury.

Here, too, you'll find the recently restored **Rudolf Gallery**. Prague's last emperor, Rudolf II was a passionate collector of exotic and idiosyncratic objects, such as stuffed animals, alchemists' tools and

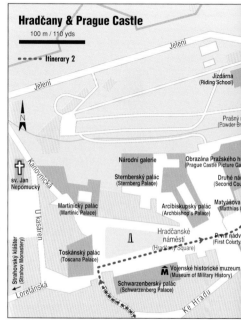

Hradčany & Prague Castle

100 m / 110 yds

•••• Itinerary 2

Jeleni

Jizdárna
(Riding School)

Prašný
(Powder Br

N

Kanovnická

sv. Jan
Nepomucký

U kasáren

Národní galerie

Sternberský palác
(Sternberg Palace)

Obrazána Pražského h
(Prague Castle Picture Ga

Druhé nád
(Second Cou

Martinický palác
(Martinic Palace)

Arcibiskupský palác
(Archbishop's Palace)

Matyášova
(Matthias G

Strahovský klášter
(Strahov Monastery)

Toskánský palác
(Toscana Palace)

Hradčanské
náměstí
(Hradčany Square)

První nádv
(First Courtya

Loretánská

Schwarzenberský palác
(Schwarzenberg Palace)

Vojenské historické muzeum
(Museum of Military History)

Ke Hradu

Above: the Archbishop's Palace

shamanistic cult figures. Although the collection was decimated by war and theft, and most of the remaining items were moved to Vienna, the gallery is worth a visit. A portal in the north wing leads to the beautifully laid-out **Royal Gardens** (Královská zahrada, open weekends), now often referred to as the Presidential Gardens.

If you have energy to spare, you may want to continue on to the Renaissance edifice of the Belvedér (**Royal Summer Palace**, Královský letohrádek).

Prague's Biggest Church

From the north side of the castle's third courtyard, the impressive façade of **St Vitus' Cathedral** (Katedrála sv Víta; chapels, crypt and tower open daily 9am–5pm) confronts you. The Gothic basilica interior is, at 124 metres (407ft) long and 60 metres (197ft) wide, the largest church in Prague. It is simply breathtaking. Begun by Charles IV's architect Matthias von Arras in 1344, and continued by Peter Parler and his sons, the cathedral has lost little of its splendour over the years. But the modern stained-glass windows, which replaced the lost originals, illuminate the interior with a rather pale light that lacks the mystery one associates with old cathedrals.

Over the centuries, the cathedral has been extended and modified. There has been no new construction work since 1929. From its inception, it was not only a place of worship, but also a coronation church, a mausoleum, a witness to historical events, and the goal of nationalist pilgrimages from every corner of the country. The elaborate **St Wenceslas's Chapel**, located in the southern transept is also steeped in national history: everything in it is associated with the life and work of this sainted Bohemian prince. A stairway leads to the Chapel of the Holy Rood, and down to the remains of an early medieval church and the royal crypt, which contains the sarcophagi of Charles IV, his consorts and of several other Bohemian kings.

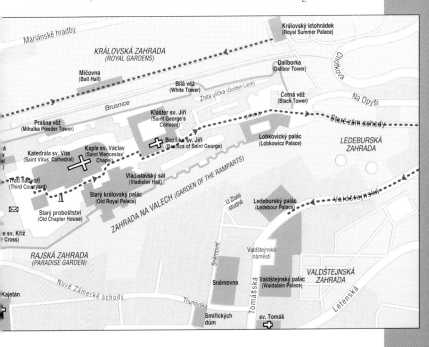

The **Old Royal Palace** (open daily 9am–5pm) opposite contains the broad and majestic **Vladislav Hall** where in bygone days mounted knights took part in tournaments. One annexe houses the **Bohemian Chancellery**, from whose windows Bohemians threw the imperial governors in 1618 *(see page 13)*. Behind the dome rises the mighty **Mihulka Tower**, the late Gothic fortification of the castle, which contains an alchemist's laboratory open to the public.

If you are ready for a break, you can get a snack in one of the many small cafés set in the castle wall behind the apse. Alternatively, wander along the much-photographed Golden Lane (Zlatá ulička, also called Goldmakers' Alley) behind **St George's Basilica** (Basilika sv Jiří, open daily 9am–5pm), where you'll find antique shops, booksellers and gift shops among the tiny, brightly coloured houses that nestle into the castle wall. Craftsmen, goldsmiths and tailors have lived and worked here for 400 years, their services available for the lords who lived next door. Here, too, you can see the **Kafka House** (No 22), which has been turned into a tiny museum.

Bohemian Dining

If you continue towards the East Gate, you will come to the observation terrace in the shadow of the **Black Tower**. From here, descend the Old Castle steps to Valdštejnská. Turning left, proceed to the Ledebour Palace (Ledeburský palác), with its small square: here, **Valdštejnská hospoda** (Valďštejnské nám 7; tel: 57 53 17 59) is the place for an authentic Bohemian meal. Alternatively, further along Tomášská on the corner of the Lesser Town Square, try **U Schnellů** (tel: 57 53 10 37). A mere 100 metres/yds away, **U Svatého Tomáše** pub (Letenská 12, tel: 53 63 65) also serves authentic cuisine.

After dinner enjoy a romantic nocturnal stroll back to your hotel.

3. WENCESLAS SQUARE
AND THE NEW TOWN *(see map p32)*

Walk from Wenceslas Square through the diverse attractions of the New Town. Then stroll along the Vltava riverbank for lunch and visits to historic churches and Charles Square. Finish the day off with a hearty Bohemian meal in U Fleků.

Start this itinerary in Wenceslas Square (metro to Můstek or Muzeum).

More of a broad avenue than an open square, Wenceslas Square was originally planned as a horse market. The square was to form the central business hub of the New Town that Charles IV was having built around the Old Town. All of Prague's historic uprisings, from the Hussite Rebellion to the Velvet Revolution, have focused on the square. It has also been the stage for national mobilisations, ignominious defeats and uproarious victory celebrations.

Today the square is the liveliest place in Prague. There are always people here – even in the early hours of the morning, the last of the night's party-goers cross paths with the city's commuters – and the smell of fresh grilled sausages is always in the air. The square is dominated by the 100-metre (328-ft) facade of the **National Museum** (Národní muzeum), constructed between 1885 and 1890. In addition to its collections of natural and national history, the museum houses a large library. The actual exhibitions are not particularly exciting, but the place is worth a visit, if only to see the busts of famous Czechs that ring the grand entrance foyer. The mighty equestrian **Statue of St Wenceslas** in the forecourt dates from 1913.

Visit the First Republic

Start your walk down the left-hand side of the 680 metre/yd long boulevard. Across the way, the Art Nouveau hotels – Evropa, Zlatá Husa and Ambassador – provide great photo material. Take a break for tea or coffee in the Evropa's grand café and you might feel as if you have stepped back into the faded grandeur of the First Republic. On this side of the square, two buildings worth seeing are the **Alfa Palace** (U Stýblů, No 28), a modernist 1920s affair, and the Art Nouveau **Peterka House** (No 12).

At the end of the square, cross over to the **Crown Palace** (Palác Koruna), which combines Constructivist and Art Nouveau elements. Heading back up the other side of the square, turn left halfway along into Jindřišská if you are still in search of refreshment. Straight ahead you'll see the imposing bell tower of the **Church of St Jindrich and St Kunhuta**, which, dating to 1350, is actually across the street. Also on this street is the recently renovated **Main Post Office**, open 24 hours with fax and parcel services.

Above Left: the Kafka House exterior. **Left:** view from the Observation Terrace
Right: riding a mechanical bull on Wenceslas Square

To the left, Panská leads down to Na příkopě, past the main office of the tourist agency **Čedok** (Na Příkopě 18; tel: 24 19 71 11).

Upscale Shopping

The lively pedestrian precinct of **Na Příkopě** is a wonderful place to indulge in some walking, people-watching and window-shopping. Here you'll find the most upscale shops and arcades in the city, including the newly reconstructed **Slovansky Dum**, complete with a state-of-the-art multiplex cinema.

To the right, towards the Powder Tower, you can book plane and train tickets in th Čedok office in the morning, obtain information from the **Prague Information Office** (No 20), or have a bite to eat along the street in the elegant Art Nouveau café of **Obecní dům**. To the left, on the opposite side of the road, you can check out the wares of two well-stocked bookshops.

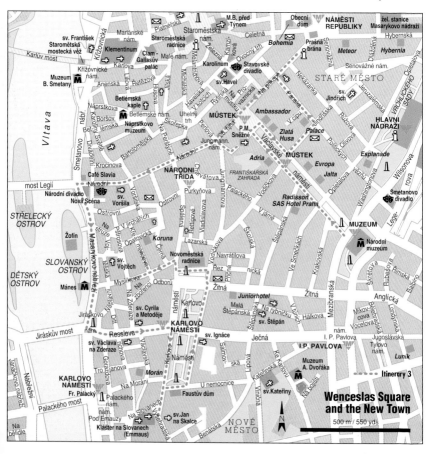

Wenceslas Square and the New Town

500 m / 550 yds

Returning to Wenceslas Square, cross the square and bear left to get to **Jungmannovo nám**, a square named after Josef Jungmann (1773–1847), who revived the Czech language. This is the site of the **Church of Our Lady of the Snows** (Kostel Panny Marie Sněžné), built in 1347. The church became famous as the headquarters of the radical Hussites who, led by Hus, marched from here to the New Town Hall in 1419 in order to teach the city's officials 'how to behave' in one of Prague's infamous defenestrations.

Bear right again to join the continuation of Na Příkopě, **Národní třída**, another lively pedestrian zone that features a modernist building now occupied by the UK supermarket Tesco, and the baroque **Church of St Ursula** (No 8). In the former **Ursuline Convent** (Klášter voršilek), you can combine art appreciation with an excellent meal in the **Convent Wine Cellar** (Klášterní vinárna; tel: 24 93 00 70, open 11.30am–midnight).

The **National Theatre** (Národní divadlo), a fine reminder of the nation's enthusiasm for culture in the late 19th century, dominates the end of the street. When the auditorium was burnt down shortly after it was completed, Prague's citizens contributed the means necessary to rebuild it within a matter of weeks. Many artists worked without payment on the magnificent decorations to ensure that its reconstruction would take place as soon as was possible. It finally opened on 18 November 1883 with a performance of Smetana's *Libuše*, the national opera. The modernist glass building of the **Nová Scéna**, designed by Karel Prager, opposite the old theatre, was opened in 1983. It became known as the **Laterna Magika** when it became the home of the leading Black Light theatre company (*see Theatre, page 90*).

The Bauhaus Influence

Heading upstream along the river, on your right you will pass **Slavic Island** (Slovanský ostrov), which has a lovely garden restaurant and a wide range of evening cultural events. Stop off at the **Mánes House** of visual arts. From the outside, the architecture of this building clearly shows the influence of Bauhaus; inside, artists' organisations present various, usually interesting, exhibitions. The beautiful café on the river entices visitors to stay awhile. If you would prefer a more hearty fish meal, continue for about 200 metres/yds past the old water tower, cross the **Jirásek Bridge** (Jiráskův most), and descend the steps to the embarkation pier of the Vltava excursion boats. Tucked away here is the little-known eatery **Vltava** (tel: 24 92 20 86), which is good for freshwater fish and a river view.

Having sated your hunger, return to the other side of the river, follow **Resslova** and turn into the second street on the right to reach the Romanesque **St Wenceslas' Church** (Kostel sv Václava na Zderaze). The name 'na Zderaze' betrays its origins as the village church of what was once a small community incorporated into the New Town. Today, somewhat anachronistically, the building serves as a home to the now inconsequential Czech Hussite Church.

Diagonally opposite, in the crypt of the Orthodox Church of **SS Cyril and Methodius** (Kostel sv Cyrila a Metoděje), a heroic sacrifice

Above Left: sculptures adorning the National Theatre
Right: a street musician with sax appeal

took place in May 1942. It was here that the resistance fighters who assassinated the SS's Reinhard 'the hangman' Heydrich took refuge from their Nazi pursuers. After fierce hand-to-hand fighting, they turned their guns on themselves rather than surrender to the enemy. The memorial that was erected here, along with a complementary exhibition that speaks volumes about the courage of the local resistance fighters, is definitely worth a visit.

Next you come to **Charles Square** (Karlovo nám), which was built during the construction of the New Town and which was once the site of the cattle market. On the right, south of some well-tended gardens, is the **Faustus House**. According to legend, this was once the residence of the German magician and alchemist Dr Faustus, famed for selling his soul to the devil in exchange for power and knowledge, but as a matter of historical fact it was the home of the English adventurer Edward Kelly, who promised Emperor Rudolf II a precious lump of gold from his alchemical laboratory.

A Rare Piece of Modern Architecture

At Vyšehradská 49, south of the square, you will find the **Emmaus Monastery** (Klášter na Slovanech) which, due to a location that controls access to the Vltava River, has played a significant role in the city since it was founded by Charles IV in 1347. A misconceived American bombing raid during World War II – the hapless pilots thought they were over Dresden – destroyed many of the monastery's irreplaceable medieval art treasures, but the magnificent cloisters alone make the place well worth a visit. The original Gothic towers were destroyed in the attack but replaced in 1969 by the distinctive, overlapping concrete curves, topped with 1.3kg (nearly 3lb) of gold. Many a tourist does a double take on seeing this modern addition to the 14th-century structure. The two sail-shaped buttresses are considered to be one of the city's few examples of original modern architecture.

Above: the U Fleků tavern is renowned for its garden, and its strong, dark beer

Head back to Charles Square, the centre of which is overshadowed by **St Ignatius Church** (Kostel sv Ignáce). This has been the Jesuits' main church in Prague since 1677. On the square's north side, the stately **New Town Hall** (Novoměstská radnice) provides an aesthetic balance to the Faustus House opposite. In 1419, the Hussite Revolution started here, as did the infamous tradition of Prague Defenestrations. Until 1784, when the five districts of Prague were amalgamated into a single administrative entity, the Town Hall remained the centre of political events in the New Town.

By now you might well be ready for dinner, in which case turn towards the **U Fleků** tavern (Křemencova 11, tel: 24 91 51 18). Go left from the Town Hall into Myslíkova, then take the second right into Křemencova. This will bring you to the famous clock that is the trademark of this renowned Old Prague inn, which is well known for its 13°-proof dark beer *(černé pivo)*. In summer a band plays in the beer garden, but you can also drink in the dim interior, which has seating for almost 1,000: either way, you should be sure to get a taste of the city's typical roast pork with dumplings.

Alternatively, turn left into Karlovo naměsti, where you will find the **U âížků** (tel: 22 23 22 57) at No 34. This restaurant also serves large helpings of traditional, well-cooked Czech food, but it is extremely popular, so you will need to make a reservation in advance. Also nearby, at Pstrossova 6, is the new location of the **Globe Bookstore and Coffeehouse**. Formerly an expatriate institution (at its previous Prague 7 location), the revamped Globe is a rather more upscale establishment that typically serves a clientele of local professionals and tourists. Free Internet terminals, fine coffee and a good selection of English books make it a popular place to pass the time.

4. THE ROYAL WAY   *(see map p22)*

A walk through the Old Town and the Lesser Town via the Royal Way.

Take the metro to Náměsti Republiky to start the walk.

'The Royal Way' became the common designation for this thoroughfare in the 14th century, when it was the shortest route between the Royal Court built by King Wenceslas IV and Prague Castle, the seat of government. Even after the kings had moved back up to the castle, processions took place along this route during coronation festivities.

Begin your tour of the Royal Way at the **Powder Tower** (Prašná brána), where the Royal Court once stood. Here you can breakfast in the ornate coffee house of the **Municipal House** (Obecní dům), the Art Nouveau building on Náměstí Republiky *(see page 25)*. Crossing Celetná, notable for its splendid baroque facades, you will come to the **Old Town Square** (Staromestské nám.) Extensive restoration work has been carried out on this section of the Royal Way and many Gothic, baroque and rococo edifices have been restored to their former glory.

Right: the Powder Tower

city itineraries

If the weather is fine, you can soak up the atmosphere of the bustling Old Town Square in one of the many outdoor cafés. In colder seasons the **Café Milena** provides a respite from the crowds gathered in front of the Old Town Hall **Astronomical Clock** (Orloj), but still affords an excellent view of the clock's procession. From here, the path leads over the Small Square (Malé náměstí) to **Karlova**, past small galleries, handicraft shops and inns. At No 18 is the **U Zlatého Hada** (At the Golden Snake) house, site of Prague's first coffee house.

After the massive **Klementinum** *(see page 46)*, the archway of the Old Town Bridge Tower affords a view of **Charles Bridge** (Karlův most). Peter Parler, Charles IV's architect, drew up the plans for this bridge in 1342, with an eye to both strategic and aesthetic concerns. Although it seems to be a direct connection between the Old Town and Malá Strana, the bridge actually has a slight S-curve; if you stand in the middle, you can't see the towers of the lower-lying bridgeheads – an effect that was intended to disconcert intruders.

A Grotesque Statue

The Old Town Bridge Tower (Staroměstská mostecká věž), dating from 1380, is meant to be the symbolic gateway into the Czech kingdom, and is a fascinating relic of the medieval imagination. Its decorations represent the medieval theory that the universe is divided into spheres. The spheres of hell, earth, moon, sun and stars are all represented by the figures that grace the surface of the tower. The tiny doorway set into the side of the tower leads to the upper floors, with beautiful views of the bridge and Hradčany Castle across the river. The winding stairway ends with a grotesque, mid-15th-century statue of a tower warden lifting his skirts to answer the call of nature. Also noteworthy is the net vaulting overhead, decorated as it is with figures of female bathing attendants in semi-transparent robes.

Over the course of several centuries, the bridge's broad sandstone balustrades were adorned with statues: today the bridge resembles an outdoor museum. And an animated museum it is. Vendors and artists sell their stuff while musicians and puppeteers entertain the passing crowds.

Above: House of the Three Violins
Right: in the Apothecary Museum

The Only Medieval Hotel

On the opposite bank of the Vltava, the Royal Way follows **Mostecká**, a busy street lined with shops. Dating from 1597, the **House of the Three Ostriches** (U tří pštrosů, Dražického náměstí 12; tel: 57 53 24 10), once the home of the supplier of imperial feathers, stands beside the bridge. This, Prague's only medieval hotel, has a fine view of the river. Mostecká runs into the **Lesser Town Square** (Malostranské náměstí), where the best place for refreshment is the coffee house **Malostranská Kavárna** (tel: 53 30 92) at No 5.

The last stretch of the Royal Way leads along picturesque **Nerudova**. Lots of little alleyways lead off this street to the stairways, nooks and crannies and tiny squares of the Lesser Town. The **Apothecary Museum** (open Apr–Sept: daily except Mon noon–6pm, from 11am Sat, Sun) recently opened at No 32. Here you can view the original interior of an 1821 apothecary's shop.

The **House of the Three Violins** (U tří housliček), easily recognised by the stucco sign with three violins hanging over its door, has a tradition of fine craftsmanship; it was for generations the residence of the renowned violin-making Edlinger family. The traditional processional route of Bohemian monarchs concludes at Prague Castle, which you can reach by climbing a steep stairwell at the end of Nerudova. To return, retrace your steps, or take Line A of the metro from Hradčanská station, which brings you back to Můstek, not far from this itinerary's starting point.

5. HIDDEN GEMS OF THE OLD TOWN *(see map p22)*

Discover the hidden delights of Staré Město, the historical Old Town.

From Staroměstská metro station walk up Kaprova Street (away from the river) then turn right to reach the Old Town Square, where this route starts.

It can be difficult following this route on a map, as many of the area's alleyways and courtyards are too tiny to be mapped at the necessary scale.

Hordes of people, particularly in the peak season, crowd into the Old Town's many cafés, restaurants, galleries and shops. Yet metres away from this hubbub, dreamy, picturesque courtyards and alleyways slumber behind old walls, hidden from tourists plying the Old Town's main routes.

Entire sections of street are linked by a labyrinth of back alleys and sequestered courtyards. Prague natives know how to take short-cuts through these passageways – it is said that one can cross town on a rainy day without getting wet. The alleyways and courtyards of this lovely city-within-a-city harbour any number of charismatic shops and characterful local bars.

Right: the Old Town's narrow streets

For your tour of this courtyard world, begin at the small entrance to the passage off Celetna 10, just a few paces from Old Town Square. Passing a few window displays, you'll find yourself on Kamzíkova Street, a narrow lane lined with dramatic crumbling walls and darkened windows. Along the way is **U Černého pava** (At the Red Peacock), a cosy restaurant offering traditional Czech meals.

A Multimedia Show of Prague's History

Turn right when you come out onto **Železná** street, walk a few metres and turn left into the inconspicuous **Kožná Street**. Follow this narrow, cobblestoned thoroughfare, which winds past pocket-sized pubs and shops, and exit on to **Melantrichova**. Across the street, a Gothic archway gives onto a once-dilapidated courtyard that has recently been spruced up and now includes a café for refreshment. Also here is **St Michael's Church**, which

hosts the 'St Michael's Mystery', a multimedia/multilingual show about Prague. Entitled the 'Prague Story', the show highlights some of the more arcane and mystical aspects of the city's history. It is shown to groups of 10 or more on Wed and Fri noon–8pm, Sat 10am–8pm. For reservations tel: 22 81 81 11, or book at the office.

Continue in the same direction and you will exit from the courtyard at the foot of **Michalská Street**. To your left, at No 20, you can fortify yourself with a glass of the Czech Republic's hearty red wine at the Michalská *vinárna*. Wine bars such as this one provide an interesting insight into the everyday life of Prague and its citizens, so it is worth stopping for a while. Once you've had your fill, cross the street and pass through the wooden gate at No 19, which leads on to an adjacent courtyard. Historians reckon that this somewhat shabby, dilapidated courtyard alley is the oldest street in the Old Town.

Back to Old Town Square

Head off through the final wooden gate and take a right turn leading on to the major street of **Jilská**. Just a few steps along, you'll come across a Gothic stone passageway leading off to your right marked 'U Kučerů', after the former residents of the house upstairs. The curving bends and ancient steps of this passage will bring you onto Hlavsova street, and then back once again to Michalska Street. From there, turn left through the wooden gateway just ahead and pass through the resonantly echoing vaulted corridor into an astonishing Renaissance courtyard, which has been brilliantly restored. Emerging into the daylight, you will find yourself back on Old Town Square – a full circle to the starting point of your journey.

Above: a street band in the Old Town maintains the city's musical traditions

6. LORETO AND THE 'NEW WORLD' *(see map p40)*

A pilgrimage to Loreto and a tour of discovery around the Nový Svĕt.

Take Line A of the metro to Hradčanská station; a five-minute walk from there will bring you to Loretánské námĕstí. Alternatively, you can take the tram: No 22 brings you to the Pohořelec stop, from which you can simply follow the route in the direction of Hradčany Castle.

The original Loreto is a place of pilgrimage in Italy. In the 13th century, angels are reputed to have brought the *Santa Casa*, the 'holy house' in which the Archangel Gabriel announced the birth of Jesus to Mary, from the Holy Land to the Italian village of Loreto. How, then, did Loreto come to Prague? Over the years, the Italian Loreto cult became popular in Bohemia, and Habsburg rulers found this legend well-suited to their purpose of returning their heretical Hussite vassals to the true faith. They therefore set about building more than 50 replicas of the 'holy house' across the land; the best known and most beautiful of these is in Prague, directly behind the castle.

The Prague Sanctuary

The **Prague Loreto** is much more than just a copy of the simple little house. Between 1626 and 1750, a large complex of buildings was thrown up here, including a chapel, multi-storeyed cloisters, the **Church of the Nativity of Our Lord**, and an early baroque tower with a carillon that dates back to 1694. In the courtyard is the **Santa Casa** (Svatá chyse) itself, built in 1626 by Giovanni Battista Orsi. Its surface is adorned with stucco reliefs depicting the lives of Old Testament prophets, the Virgin Mary and assorted saints. On the narrower side you'll find a depiction of the legend of the translocation of the Loreto Santa Casa, while a beam and several bricks from the original Italian Loreto have been incorporated into the interior.

The sanctuary's biggest attraction is the **Loreto Treasury** (open daily except Mon, 9am–12.15pm, 1–4pm), which was built to accommodate the many valuable offerings – including jewelled goblets – that have been placed at the statue of the Virgin Mary. One such monstrance weighs some 12kg (26lb), and is set with over 6,000 diamonds.

Opposite the entrance and behind the Santa Casa, make your way towards the **Church of the Nativity** (Kostel Narození Páne), built in 1734 on the site of the original Chapel of St Anne. The exceptional architecture is complemented by equally exquisite interior decorations. The vaulted ceiling is graced by a fresco of the Crucifixion by Václav Vavrinec Reiner, one of Prague's most renowned artists.

Right: the Church of the Nativity

Opposite the church, you can hardly miss the monumental facade of the **Černín Palace** (Černínský Palác). Originally, the great Italian architect Gianlorenzo Bernini was commissioned to design the building, but a quarrel with Count Černín resulted in Bernini withdrawing from the project. The palace was ultimately built by Italian workmen in the Italian style. Damaged in the 18th century, it has been restored more than once since then and now houses the Foreign Affairs Ministry. It is not open to the public.

If you're hungry at this point, one of Prague's best-loved pubs is a stone's throw away. **At the Black Bull** (U cerneho vola), situated on Loretánské námestí, is a former knight's hall serving some of the best beer and garlic soup in the city. What's more, profits from the pub go towards the school for the blind located next door.

Artists in Search of Patrons

Next on this itinerary is the 'New World' – a translation of the street name Nový Svět. The original residents of this little alley off Loreto Square were once the poorest people of Hradčany. Today the tiny houses with their pocket-sized gardens, lovingly restored, are homes to artists hoping to be discovered by wealthy tourists. No 1, the **'Golden Horn'** (U zlatého rohu), was once home of the astronomer Johann Kepler. The violinist Frantisek Ondricek, the composer Rudolf Friml, and the Danish astronomer Tycho Brahe all lived on the street. If you haven't had lunch, the **Golden Pear** winery (U zlaté hrušky) at Nov´y Svět 3 (daily 11.30am–3pm, 6.30pm–midnight; tel: 20 51 47 78) is a good option.

A few paces away is **Galerie Novy Svet** (Novy Svet 5; daily 10am–6pm), displaying works by the country's 20th-century masters as well as promising young artists. The gallery's owners are on hand to explain the significance of the exhibits in the context of Czech art.

Loreta and the Strahov Monastery

400 m / 440 yds

Above: in the Church of the Nativity
Right: the Theological Room

7. STRAHOV MONASTERY *(see map p40)*

A visit to one of the most beautiful historic libraries in Europe.

Taking Line A of the metro to Malostranská station, transfer to tram No 22 or 23 and go to the Pohořelec stop; alternatively proceed from the underground station on foot (a walk of about 15 minutes).

Strahov Monastery (Strahovský klášter, Strahovské nádvoří 1, open daily except Mon 9am–5pm; tel: 20 51 66 95) sits on the slope of **Petřín Hill**. Built in 1143, the monastery is scarred by history: it was burnt down in 1258, and damaged in the Hussite and Thirty Years' wars and by a French bombardment in 1742. It was occupied by the Prussian army in the centuries that followed. Additions and modifications during the early Gothic, Renaissance, and baroque periods have left the original Romanesque elements evident only in the **Church of the Annunciation of Our Lady**.

The monastery has one of the most beautiful and extensive libraries in Europe. The core of the collection, comprising more than 130,000 volumes including 2,500 first editions, was formed in the mid-18th century. Many monasteries were dissolved in Joseph II's reign, and Strahov's abbot seized the opportunity to purchase many valuable collections. Further additions from the libraries of defunct monasteries came after World War II.

Literary Highlights

The library's highlights are the 10th-century *Strahov Gospel Book* (a copy is on display; the original is locked away) and a first edition of Copernicus's *De Revolutionibus Orbium Coelestium* (1543), in which he first expounded his heliocentric theory of the universe. The library's two ornate rooms are impressive. Both the **Theological Room**, with baroque ceiling frescoes, a small, barred cabinet containing books once banned by Church censors and a 17th-century globe from the Netherlands, and the **Philosophical Hall** are open to the public (Tues–Sun 9am–5pm). Beyond its actual contents, the Philosophical Hall is distinctive due to its richly carved and gilded walnut cabinets. Elaborate ceiling frescoes by the rococo painter Anton Maulpertsch celebrate the accord of philosophy, science and religion. Today the library also serves as the **Czech Literary Museum**, whose archives contain some 3 million items, including the works of some 1,200 Czech authors.

8. ENCHANTING VYŠEHRAD (see map p43)

A visit to the legendary birthplace of the Czech nation.

Take Line C of the metro to the Vyšehrad station starting point.

Vyšehrad is a rocky hill that rises from the place where the Vltava reaches the old city limits. According to legend it was here, in her father's castle, that Princess Libuše had her vision of the golden city of Prague: 'I see a great city, whose fame will reach to the stars… there in the woods you shall build your castle and your settlement, which shall be named Praha.'

Archaeologists doubt the veracity of this tale – Prague Castle was built in the 9th century; Vyšehrad was erected in the 10th century. But in the second half of the 19th century, at the peak of the Czech national revival, the story was irresistible to the likes of Smetana and Mendelssohn-Bartholdy, and it formed the basis of their operas *Libuše* and *Libussa's Prophecy*.

Vyšehrad (literally 'high castle') has played a key role in Prague's history since the Přemyslid kings established it as their seat of power. Its tumultuous career as a battle fortress began in 1004, when it repelled the invading forces of Poland's Boleslav the Brave. Over the years the royal residence alternated between Vyšehrad and Hradčany, and the hill was repeatedly ransacked by foreign armies. Today by contrast Vyšehrad features idyllic tree-lined paths.

Leaving the metro you will pass the imposing Congress Centre, formerly known as the Palace of Culture, before you come to the **Tábor Gate** and the ruins of 14th-century fortifications. Passing through the gate, you'll come upon an **Information Centre** (open daily 9.30am–5pm), souvenir shop and small café on your right. Here it's possible to book tours of the **underground casements** built by the French during their occupation in the 18th century. The tunnels have four of the original statues from the Charles Bridge.

St Peter's Intervention

Ahead is the 17th-century Leopold Gate and, to the right, the tiny Romanesque St Martin's Rotunda. From here, take a left onto K Rotunde Street with its low stone walls. Along this quiet street you'll pass a lawn on your right where three short stone columns lean against each other at odd angles. This is **The Devil's Pillar**. Locals will tell you that a priest bet the devil that he could say Mass before the devil could deliver a column from St Peter's Basilica in Rome. The devil took a column from a closer church, but St Peter intervened, waylaying the devil and breaking the pillar in three. According to the legend, those pieces are what we see today.

Further on is the well-tended Vyšehrad Park and the **Church of Saints Peter and Paul**, whose interior features Art Nouveau paintings of saints. There has been a church here since the 11th century, but the present twin-spired neo-Gothic church dates to 1885. Nearby lies the 1870 **Vyšehrad Cemetery**, which is the resting place of numerous national figures, including the composers Smetana and Dvořák, the writers Jan Neruda and Karel Čapek, and the artist Alfons Mucha. A great pantheon, the Slavín, honours them all.

Left: visit the great composer's resting place

city itineraries

Legendary Statues

Most visitors to Vyšehrad walk across the park towards the fortifications overlooking the river. Pass through the stone gate opposite the cemetery and you will enter a wide lawn graced with four monumental statues by the celebrated sculptor Jan Myslbek. The statues depict characters from Czech legends that so often feature Vyšehrad, including Libuse herself. Further along, in the former summer palace of Emperor Charles IV, the **Vyšehrad Gallery** (Apr–Nov: open daily 9.30am–7pm) has a fine collection of landscapes and prints inspired by this hill's majesty.

Continuing your stroll along the battlements, you will be treated to a wonderful panorama of the city's southern expanses, as the Vltava winds its way into the wooded hills in the distance. The remnants of buildings jutting out of the rock were once the outpost towers from which sentinels kept watch over the Vltava. The city had to be alert to the perennial threat of invasion by powerful enemies' armies.

Turn back towards the cathedral and you will find refreshments available at the **Na Vyšehradě** restaurant, which has a spacious outdoor dining area for use in warm weather. From here, either return to the metro or walk down Vratislavova Street to the embankment to catch tram No 17 back to the city centre.

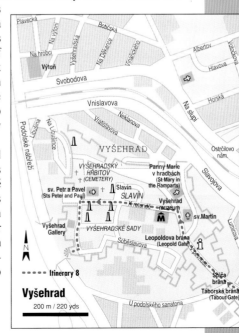

Above: the castle's cemetery

9. GREEN PRAGUE *(see map p22)*

A day of rest and recreation on Petřin Hill and in Letná Park.

From the National Theatre, tram No 22 travels over the river to Helichova station (two stops away) in the Lesser Town. Opposite the station, follow the signs to the Lanová draha, which will bring you to the funicular; now decide whether to ascend Petřin by cable car or on foot (the funicular runs daily every 20 mins from 8am to 6pm; regular transit tickets are valid).

Letná Park and **Petřín Hill** constitute Prague's largest green spaces. They are located either side of Hradčany Castle. If you decide to hike up the hill, the path will lead you through fruit orchards which in the spring are enlivened by a beautiful mass of blossoms. The beginning of the walk is marked with a monument to the writer Jan Neruda (1834–91). Park benches en route offer both ample opportunites for rest and, after a few hundred metres, lovely views out over Prague.

Above the cable car's first stop, the terrace café of the extensive **Vinárna Nebozízek** (tel: 57 31 53 29, open daily 11am–6pm, 7–11pm) attracts a great many visitors en route to the summit. From here, too, you can enjoy a wonderful panoramic view over the opposite bank. Should you want to eat in this winery, you ought to reserve a table in advance.

A Replica of the Eiffel Tower

On the hill, where the cable car ends its journey, a few recommended sights await. Children in particular enjoy the **Maze** (Bludiště, summer only: Tues–Sun 9.30am–5pm). For a view of really distant places, check out the **Observatory** (Hvězdárna, open Mon–Fri 6–8pm, Sat, Sun 10am–noon, 2–8pm). The **Observation Tower** (Rozhledna, Tues–Sun 9.30am–5pm), a scale replica of the Eiffel Tower, has been open to the public since 1991.

Having seen the best of the park, and its views of the city, you must again choose whether to descend by cable car or wear out some more shoe leather. Several paths lead through a small wood to the foot of Petřín Hill. If you bear to the left, you come to the grounds of the **Strahov Monastery**.

A visit to Petřín Hill can be combined with a trip to the monastery, the **Loreto Sanctuary** and **Hradčany**, or you might opt to wander through the

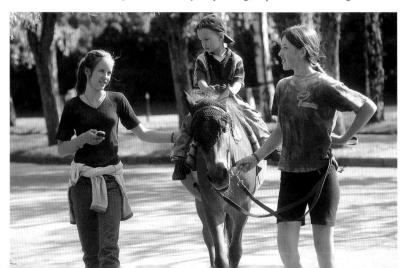

picturesque alleyways of the Lesser Town. Alternatively you could roam through the court gardens of **Na Valech** and **Rajská** (Paradise), or even the **Royal Garden** (Kralovská zahrada). Ferdinand I sacrificed several vineyards in order to create the Royal Garden in 1534. It was he who had the Royal Summer Palace built there.

You could then round off your visit with a walk through **Letná Park**, which extends along the crest of a long hill to **Štefanikův Bridge**. A platform above the river supported a massive memorial to Stalin until 1962 and now affords good views of the city. Not far away is the Art Nouveau pavilion known as the **Hanavský Pavilion**, which was designed for the 1891 Jubilee Exhibition and which today houses a romantic restaurant. Also in the vicinity of Letná Park you'll find the **Sparta Stadium** and several ice-hockey rinks.

10. Along the Vltava *(see map p22)*

Explore the various museums and cafés along the banks of the river.

Take metro line A to Staromětská station; turn left towards Charles Bridge.

Many visitors, overwhelmed by Prague's architectural majesty, overlook the true heart of the city – the Vltava River. Known by some as the Moldau, this humble but lyrical river makes a graceful S-curve through the city and has stood as a silent witness to centuries of Bohemian history. Its place in the nation's heart was assured by Smetana's symphonic poem *The Vltava*.

Begin your day at the **Smetana Museum** (Novotného lavka; open daily except Tues, 10am–noon, 12.30–5pm; tel: 24 22 90 75), where you will find a small and tempting café for a late breakfast. The museum is situated on a small spit of land, just past Charles Bridge, housed in an attractive Neo-Renaissance building that used to be the municipal waterworks, and is definitely worth a visit. On the first floor, documents and objects illustrate the life and work of Bedřich Smetana (1824–84) who is known as the father of Czech music, and whose spirit seems virtually omnipresent in Prague.

A few steps back in the direction from which you came will bring you to the **Square of the Knights of the Cross** (Křizovnické náměstí), and back into the

Left: pony ride on the hill
Above: tunnel of love. **Right:** on the Vltava

tourist scene. Cross the square to enter the **Gallery of the Knights of the Cross**, the repository for treasures that the Order of the Knights of the Cross with the Red Star has amassed over the centuries. Still extant, this is the only male order in the history of the Catholic Church founded by a female, St Agnes of Bohemia, daughter of King Premysl Otakar I, in 1237.

Inside, you will find a small but noteworthy collection of European paintings, from Gothic altar panels to 19th-century landscapes, as well as the ruins of the Judith Bridge – the predecessor of the Charles Bridge. The bejewelled monstrances, chalices and reliquaries of the treasure room give a good idea of the order's wealth; conversely, a chapel that dates to the 13th-century is a tribute to the order's history of religious devotion.

Weapons of the Counter-Reformation

On leaving the gallery, look to the left to see the sprawling complex known as the **Klementinum**. Despite its great size, the Klementinum frequently goes unnoticed by visitors and guides, while nearby Charles Bridge occupies everyone's attention. And yet this former Dominican monastery, which was taken over by Jesuits in the 16th century, is excellent testimony to the way in which the Jesuits, who spearheaded the Counter-Reformation, prepared themselves for the war on heresy. A school, library, printing press and theatre demonstrate that these 'warriors', who are often accused of converting Protestants by force of arms, were quite prepared to fall back on more learned methods of persuasion. The Klementinum houses the **State Library** (no fixed opening hours, visits by arrangement), whose collection could keep you occupied for hours – note, for instance, the collection of globes in the Mathematics Hall. Concerts are frequently held in the Klementinum's Chapel of Mirrors – you might be offered handbills advertising these events.

Continue along Křižovnická Street and you will arrive at **Jana Palacha námůstí**, a square devoted to the memory of Jan Palach, a student who immolated himself in protest against the Soviet oppression of the 20th century. The square is dominated by the **Rudolfinum**, with its statues of the pantheon of Central European composers ranged along the roof. Built as the first Czech parliament building in the latter days of the Austro-Hungarian empire, today it serves as a concert hall and home of the Czech Philharmonic.

Facing the river, you'll find the entrance to the **Rudolfinum Gallery** (open daily except Mon

Above: the Klementinum, focus of the Counter-Reformation
Right: St Agnes was canonised in 1989

10am–6pm) guarded by twin sphinxes. The gallery features large-scale exhibitions throughout the year. Before entering the gallery, take in the view of the Vltava's opposite bank from one of the benches dotted along the embankment. The imposing buildings around the square belong to the school's philosophy faculty, and this area is a popular spot for students, and the odd professor, relaxing between lectures.

Just a few steps down the street at 17 Listopadu Street 2 is the **Museum of Decorative Arts** (open daily except Mon 10am–6pm; tel: 51 09 31 11), which features a fascinating permanent exhibition of jewellery, furniture and design and hosts various relevant temporary exhibitions. The museum's gift shop is a surprisingly good place if you're looking for souvenirs – check out its selection of silk, porcelain, jewellery and print items.

After many years of restoration work, the **Convent of St Agnes** (Anežský klášter, U milosrdných 17, Prague 1, open daily except Mon 10am–6pm; tel: 21 87 91 11) was reopened to the public in 1980. The Agnes to whom it is dedicated was the sister of Wenceslas I and the first abbess of the convent. Agnes introduced the Order of the Poor Clares into Bohemia and was canonised in 1989. Part of this complex houses the National Gallery's collection of medieval Czech art. Conclude your Vltava walk on the **Botel Albatros**, further upstream on the embankment. From the terrace café of this permanently anchored floating hotel you can enjoy a drink while viewing the city of Prague and its river from a different angle.

11. ŽIŽKOV *(see map p48)*

A walk through one of Prague's most characterful quarters. After lunch at the top of the space-age Television Tower, visit the Military History Museum, and a republican monument that was transformed into a communist mausoleum.

Walk from metro line A's Jiřího z Poděbrad station.

Îiľkov, a lively, working-class quarter with lots of atmosphere, has long been one of Prague's best-loved neighbourhoods. Its buildings and streets may be a bit dingy, but their patina holds such a powerful residue of historical charm that it can seem as if you're strolling through a 19th-century daguerreotype.

Emerging from the metro, you will find yourself on Náměstí Jiřího z Poděbrad, the main feature of which is the monumental **Church of the Sacred Heart** with its distinctive, tombstone-shaped clock tower. This fascinating church was built by a Slovenian architect in 1932, and is intended to have intimations of Noah's ark.

Behind the church, turn left on Milešovská Street and you might be shocked by the gargantuan appearance of the somewhat surreal **Television Tower** looming above you. Construction began in the communist

Right: the Television Tower

era and was completed not long after 1989's Velvet Revolution. The tower broadcasts radio, television and mobile phone signals.

For 120 Kč, you can ascend 93 metres (305ft) of the 216-metre (709ft) tower to the **observation deck**. There, you will be treated to an unparalleled view of Prague and its environs; on a clear day, visibility stretches for distances up to 100km (62 miles). For lunch, drop down one level and dine at 65 metres (213ft) above the street in the luxurious **Tower Restaurant**. The observation deck and restaurant are open daily, 10am–11pm.

Walk downhill to Husitská Street, past a plethora of working-class pubs and bars: **Restaurace Morava** at Bořivojova 96 is typical. At Husitská, turn left and proceed to the foot of the hill behind, and the right-hand pavement, which leads to the summit of **Vítkov Hill**, site of the **National Monument**, built to honour World War I soldiers. The communists turned the building into a **mausoleum** for their leaders, and built the **statue of Jan Žižka**, the Hussite military leader. This is the largest equestrian statue in the world.

12. VÝSTAVIŠTĚ *(see map p18–19)*

Enjoy the Exhibition Grounds, focusing on the Great Hall, stroll round the former Imperial Hunting Grounds, and take a tour through a stunning 17th-century chateau.

Take tram 12, 17 or 5 to the Výstaviště stop just north of the centre.

Ask any Praguer to recommend a good place at which to while away a sunny afternoon, and they'll probably send you to a part of the city that

royalty and ordinary citizens alike have been enjoying for centuries. Whether you fancy a quiet stroll through a picturesque park, family fun in a carnival setting, or a dose of high culture, Výstaviště is the best place to be.

Výstaviště (Prague's Exhibition Grounds) have played an active role in the city's cultural life since it was built to accommodate the 1891 Jubilee Industrial Exhibition. Physically, the complex focuses on the whimsical **Great Hall**, a popular venue for trade fairs, concerts and special events. But the real show takes

Left: eyes on the action at the Exhibition Grounds
Right: family fun in a carnival setting

place to the rear, at the famous **Křižík Fountain**, designed by the electrical pioneer František Křižík. The fountain comprises hundreds of individually controlled jets and lights, and when set to music – anything from Dvořák to the Three Tenors – it makes an impressive spectacle. Shows take place daily at 6, 7 and 8pm.

Celebrating Shakespeare

The Exhibition Grounds house a replica of Shakespeare's Globe Theatre, which sometimes stages performances in English, and also the National Museum's **Lapidarium** (open Tues–Fri noon–6pm, Sat, Sun 10am–6pm). This collection preserves the nation's heritage through the conservation of stone statues and architectural treasures from across the country. These include several of the original Charles Bridge statues. While you're in the Exhibition Grounds, look for one of the many **carnivals** that take place there throughout the year. With Ferris wheels, roller coasters and lots of music, they are hard to miss.

On leaving the Exhibition Grounds, you're well placed to take a stroll around the neighbouring **Stromovka Park** – an enormous wooded area filled with flowery paths that formerly served as the **Imperial Hunting Grounds**. First established in the 13th century, the grounds enjoyed their heyday under the Habsburg kings, and were opened to the public in 1804. Today, located well away from the noise and pollution of the city streets, Stromovka Park can easily persuade you that you're not in a capital city at all.

Keeping to the left-hand path, make the (slow) ascent to the **Governor's Summer Palace** (Místodržitelský letohrádek). This, the hunting lodge of King Ladislav Jagellon, which was later rebuilt in English neo-Gothic style, towers over the park. If you're there on a Wednesday, you can tour the building, which now houses a branch of the National Museum library.

Descending into the park proper, the ruin you see below and to the right is the old **Royal Hall**. Built as a leisure pavilion in the 17th century, the hall served as a restaurant for the Communist Party elite until it was burnt

down in 1979. Today it is known as Šlechta Restaurant. Also of interest in Stromovka is the **Planetarium** (Hvězdárna, open daily except Fri 9.30am–8pm, shows usually start at 6pm), which regularly hosts laser and astronomical shows as well as other popular forms of entertainment.

Leaving the park, follow signs for the 'Zoo' and 'Troja' through the rose gardens, across the river and past the horse farm until you come to the stately **Troja Chateau** (Trojský zámek, open Apr–Oct: daily except Mon 10am–6pm; Nov–Mar: Sat, Sun only 10am–5pm). The chateau was the result of the Czech nobleman Václav Vojtěch of Šternberk's ambitions to increase his influence over Prague Castle by building the finest baroque country house north of the Alps. He assumed that, after hunting in Stromovka, the emperor would be unable to resist feasting in this wedding cake of a building.

Before entering the chateau you might want to pause for lunch. Two tempting restaurants are located right in front of the chateau's main gate. If you fancy simple, hearty Czech pub fare, the rustic **Restaurace U Lišků** should suit. For a slightly more upscale affair, try the **Rudolf III** opposite. Both establishments serve a fine mug of Czech beer.

Celebration of the Olympic Gods

The Troja Chateau, completed in 1685, made considerable demands on the skills of the architect, who had to build it on a special support ramp so that it would face Prague Castle. Its most striking feature is the monumental double staircase featuring depictions of Olympic gods celebrating victory. Look below to see the defeated Titans whom they have just cast into the underworld. A tour of the chateau is definitely worthwhile. In addition to its permanent collection of 19th-century Czech paintings and sculpture, it houses a fascinating exhibition of firearms, some dating from the 15th century. Period costumes and furniture are also on display.

The **Great Hall** frequently astonishes visitors with the brilliant three-

Above: the Troja chateau, possibly the finest baroque country house this side of the Alps

dimensional illusions created in its frescoes by the Italian brothers Francesco and Giovanni Marchetti. (Look for the figures of these remarkable craftsmen peering out from a gap between the painted pillars.) The chapel contains a valuable collection of treasures including monstrances and jewellery. Also worth noting are the **Chinese rooms**. The lord of the house had a fondness for all things Oriental, and these rooms contain authentic Chinese panels and vases worked in exquisite detail.

The chateau's expansive Italian garden, with its striking array of remarkable terracotta vases, busts and allegories, may have already caught your eye. The harmony created between chateau and garden is striking, especially considering the labyrinthine baroque orchard to the side. The overall effect is one of a refined opulence and quiet charm unique in this area. Wine has been grown here for centuries, and indeed, perched above the vineyards behind the chateau you can find the **Chapel of St Clare**, patron saint of vintners.

You might conclude your day, especially if you have children, with a visit to the **Prague Zoo** (tel: 688 1800 for opening times, which vary during the course of the year, and for special events) just opposite the chateau's main entrance. To return to the centre of Prague, take bus 112 from outside the chateau gate to the metro station at Nadraží Holešovice.

13. BÍLÁ HORA *(see map p18–19)*

Take a trip that encompasses sightseeing – at the Břevnov monastery, the Hvězda summer palace and an historic battleground – a walk through a wooded nature preserve, and a taste of fine Czech beer in an atmospheric tavern that was once a monastery.

Take the tram, either No 8 or No 22, in the direction of the 'Bílá Hora' terminal; you will find a cluster of interesting sights on the city's western edge.

If you're ready for a reprieve from the hustle and bustle of the city centre, Bílá Hora, on the western edge of the city, is the ideal destination. Our first stop is the venerable **Břevnov Monastery**, or Břevnovský klášter. Founded in 993, this, Bohemia's first monastery, served as a base for the Benedictine order in Central Europe. In keeping with the turbulent course of Czech history, the monastery's fortunes rose and fell over the ensuing centuries: it was burnt down and ransacked

Above: a feeding flamingo at the zoo
Right: outside the Brevnov monastery

several times by the various foreign forces that overran the city. Under the communists the monastery suffered from 40 years of neglect from which it is still recovering.

A Tour of the Monastery

Pass through the gate decorated with a statue of St Benedict and enter the spacious courtyard and gardens, which are overshadowed by the baroque **St Margaret Basilica** (Basilika sv. Markéty), built between 1703 and 1715 and now restored to its original pristine beauty. The six altar paintings by Petr Brandl are of particular interest. The monastery also houses a somewhat eerie 11th-century **Romanesque Crypt**, which was only recently discovered by archaeologists. Similarly worth seeing is the **Abbot's Residence**, which features the stately **Theresian Hall**. Named in honor of a visit by the Empress Maria Theresa, the hall's highlight is probably the picturesque late-baroque ceiling frescoes. Guided tours of the basilica, crypt and residence are available on Saturdays and Sundays at 10am and 2pm.

If you are ready for refreshments, stop at the homely **U Kláštera** restaurant (open daily 10am–11pm) across the street; it serves all the standard

Czech specialities. A short ride two stations further down the tram line, to the Vypich stop, brings you to a wide grassy expanse. Cross this and pass through the white stone gate to enter an idyllic wooded **nature preserve**. Founded in 1534 by King Ferdinand I as Prague's second royal hunting grounds, the area is now a popular spot with locals. You are bound to see families and amorous couples enjoying a leisurely stroll among the woods' towering beeches and oaks.

A Secret Wife's Hideaway

Immediately at the end of a broad, tree-lined promenade you will see the appropriately named **Letohrádek Hvězda** (Star Summer Palace). This singular, six-pointed construction – reputedly the only one of its type in the world – was designed and built by the Archduke Ferdinand of Tyrol in 1555 as a hideaway for his secret wife, the allegedly very beautiful Filipina Welser. The educated and enlightened archduke brought to the building his appreciation of art, and today the palace houses a wonderful collection of 16th–18th-century European graphic art, including works by Dürer, Goya and Rembrandt. The exhibition is open May–Sept: daily except Mon 9am–5pm; Oct–Apr: daily except Mon 10am–4pm.

When you have finished wandering through the wooded paths around the palace, return to the tram line and ride two more stops to the **Bílá Hora** (White Mountain) terminus. A short walk uphill through the adjacent neighbourhood will bring you to the peak of the 'mountain', better described as a hillock. The summit, such as it is, is crowned by a **memorial** to the soldiers who were killed at the Battle of White Mountain in 1620. In that battle the

Above: pausing for breath. **Above Right:** the Star Summer Palace. **Right:** the Brevnov monastery features an array of architectural styles

Protestant Czech lords were roundly vanquished by the Habsburg army, a defeat that led to three centuries of German hegemony over Bohemia. When the weather permits, the 'mountain' affords a stunning vista of the surrounding countryside.

If you have worked up an appetite after all of the walking, backtrack to the tram stop and find a seat in the historic **Velká hospoda** (Great Tavern), where you'll be treated to a superb selection of Czech specialities. Here you can reflect over a frothy mug of Czech beer in the very courtyard where monks once meditated: the pub owes it unique atmosphere to the fact that it was originally built as a chapel and monastery after the battle by the victorious Emperor Ferdinand II.

Final Resting Place

It was not very long before the chapel and monastery were deemed an insufficient commemoration of the great military victory, and Ferdinand commissioned the **Church of Our Lady Victorious** (open Sun 10am–noon, Thur 4.30–6pm only), located just across the road. This tiny, charming chapel is a true gem, built by the greatest Czech baroque architect, Jan Blažej Santini, on the site of a former chapel and ossuary containing the remains of the White Mountain warriors. If you still have energy to burn, you could take a final stroll through the grounds of the surrounding **Servite Monastery** before catching the tram back to the city centre.

city itineraries

Excursions

1. KARLŠTEJN *(see map p56)*

To reach the town of Karlštejn by car, take the E50 towards Plzeň (Pilsen), and exit at Loděnice; or the E50 to Beroun, exiting at Srbsko-Karlštejn; or Street 4 towards Dobřís, turning off before Zbraslav in the direction of Dobřichovice-Karlštejn (35km/22 miles). Alternatively, take metro line B to Smíchovské nádraží, then a train to Karlštejn station.

Trains leave regularly for Karlštejn from Prague's main railway station starting at 8.11am. The journey takes about 45 minutes.

If you took the express train from Germany to Prague via Plzeň, some 30km (19 miles) from Prague you might catch a glimpse of a stony cliff crowned by a castle as it briefly emerges in a narrow valley between two hills. This is **Karlštejn Castle** (open daily 9am–noon, 1–4pm; Apr and Oct: till 5pm, May, June and Sept: till 6pm, July and Aug: till 7pm; tel: 0311 681 617. Admission is limited so book ahead for a reservation). The most attractive excursion site in the Prague region, it draws countless tourists every year.

The castle was built by Charles IV between 1348 and 1357, with massive walls to protect his many religious relics and worldly treasures. In those days, the most valuable imperial relics – a crystal container with a tooth supposedly from the mouth of John the Baptist, an arm of St Anne, a golden imperial orb, a silver sceptre and the like – were publicly exhibited once a year, on the 'Day of Relics' (the Friday after Easter). Today, after a period of nearly 20 years during which the castle was closed for restoration, visitors can view all these treasures as well as some of the finest frescoes in the world in Karlštejn's **Chapel of the Holy Cross**.

The Czech Republic's Greatest Treasure

The chapel is the Czech Republic's answer to the Sistine Chapel, and perhaps its greatest artistic and cultural treasure. During the reign of Holy Roman Emperor Charles IV, it could arguably have laid claim to the title of the spiritual centre of Europe. The completion of its renovations has restored it to its rightful place among the most illustrious medieval sanctuaries on the continent. Gold walls and ceilings are embedded with precious jewels, the vaulted ceiling has 32 Venetian-glass stars. The celebrated frescoes of the saints and apostles by Master Theodoric date to the 1360s. A visit to the castle does involve a steep climb, but at least the path from Karlštejn is lined with cafés, restaurants and souvenir shops.

Most of the open rooms of the castle proper are located in the south-facing palace section. Here you'll find an enormous **Audience Hall** as well as the **Imperial Bedroom**. To the north of the palace

Left: the castle towers over the town
Right: statue of St Catherine in the castle

you can explore the imposing **Marian Tower**, which houses Charles IV's private residential quarters as well as the **Church of Our Lady**, which incorporates the emperor's personal **St Catherine Chapel**. At the heart of the complex lies the **Great Tower**, where the royal treasures and holy relics, whose protection was the castle's original *raison d'être*, were kept.

A Prehistoric Rhino

While in the area, you might want to combine a visit to the castle with a ramble around Karlštejn. **Bohemian Karst** (Český Kras) and the **Karlštejn Forest** conceal a number of small lakes suitable for a picnic or a paddle on a hot summer's day. If you are looking to avoid the rain, or indeed the heat of the sun, the nearby **Koneprusy Caves** (open daily May–Sept: 8am–4pm, Oct: until 2pm; closed in winter) make for a cool, and fascinating escape.

This subterranean attraction, situated some 6km (4 miles) south of Beroun, reaches depths of 600m (1,950ft) and is full of colourful formations, to say nothing of its human bones and prehistoric woolly rhinoceros. You'll also find a 15th-century forge designed to make counterfeit coins.

On your way back to the capital, it's a good idea to ask locals to point out the scenic route along the **Berounka River**. The trip may take a few minutes longer, but once you glimpse this beautiful valley and the sparkling river that winds through it, you are unlikely to regret taking this detour.

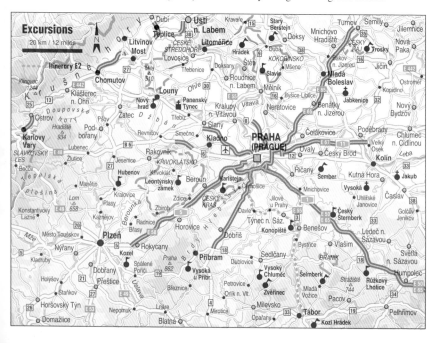

2. TÁBOR TO THE VLTAVA *(see map p56)*

An expedition to the Hussite stronghold of Tábor, and Castle Konopiště

By car, go southeast from Prague along the Euroroute E55 towards České Budějovice and Linz. Return to Prague along the romantic upper course of the Vltava via the E55 to Benešov and Konopiště. Alternatively, trains leave regularly for Tábor from Prague's main train station, starting at 8.58am. The journey takes about an hour and a half.

In Prague, the image of Jan Hus, the God-fearing pastor and vigorous opponent of ostentation and bigotry, whose influence dominated an entire epoch of Czech history, remains oddly blurred. In **Tábor**, however, everything is a reminder of the Hussites' heyday. The Bible (Matthew 17, I–IX) tells us that Mount Tabor was the site of Jesus's transfiguration. The Hussites had this in mind when in 1420, five years after the execution of their leader and only a few months after the Prague rebellion, thousands of them – men, women and children – gathered near Castle Kozí hrádek to march against the imperial army and Catholic bigotry. Their enormous camp had to be stocked with provisions, and fortified against possible attack by the Catholic enemy, and thus the new settlement of Tábor came into being.

From Tábor began the campaign whose high point was a glorious victory at Vítkov Hill in 1420. However, after the fall of the brilliant military commander Field Marshal Jan Žižka in 1424, the struggle met a bitter end in the defeat near Lipany in 1434. The Hussite dream of a Bohemian religious nation free of the corruption of the Catholic Church was not to be fulfilled.

The Black Flag with the Red Goblet

After the war, Tábor blossomed into a prosperous city, in which adherents of all faiths, including Catholics, were tolerated. Yet the spirit of rebellion remained very much alive; whenever revolts against serfdom and usury broke out anywhere in Bohemia, Tábor's citizens were quick to fly the black

flag emblazoned with a red goblet to show their solidarity with the rebels. Defeat at the Battle of White Mountain in 1620 brought the city's independence to an end, and thereafter Tábor had to pay fealty to the Catholic Habsburgs.

To explore Tábor, leave the Euroroute, turn right and leave your car in the car park near the castle ruins. From there, you can proceed directly to the mighty **Round Tower** and the **Bechyně Gate**, with its small historical exhibition.

Narrow, winding streets lined with run-down little houses lead up to Žižka Square, which is honeycombed – like virtually all of the city – with secret defensive passageways and military storerooms, mostly dating from the Hus-

Above Left: Chapel of the Virgin Mary, one of many in the castle
Right: the town of Tábor, formerly a Hussite stronghold

site era. Ever since the Czech nationalist movement proudly adopted the Hussites as their forerunners in the 19th century, a monumental **statue** of the leaders of the Hussite army has adorned this broad square. **Roland's Fountain** stands here, too, as well as two simple stone tables that were once used during the community's open-air communion services.

The high tower of the **Church of the Transfiguration of Our Lord** (Chrám Proměnění Páně na hoře Tábor), which dates from the Hussite era, towers over the former **Town Hall** with its splendid city arms and two-storey council room, now containing a museum dedicated to the Hussite movement. Nearby, an old residential residence has been converted into a rustic regional restaurant, with tables set out in the square in summer.

A walk through Prážská ulice and the side streets leading off it will take

you past various studios, galleries, antique shops and bookstores. Before you reach the well-preserved city wall to the north, you can see **Jordan Pond**, which was first dammed for use as the city's water reservoir in 1492. Definitely worth taking some time to see is the **Hussite Museum** (Iizkovske namesti 2, open daily Apr–Sept: 9am–6pm, Nov–Mar 10am–4pm), which exhibits Hussite artefacts and which conducts tours of the catacombs beneath the square.

The stone **Kotnov Castle tower** offers a wonderful view of a town that is punctuated throughout with handsome Renaissance houses and such baroque monuments as the **Monastery of the Virgin Mary**. If all of this history has whetted your appetite for the kind of hearty Central European cuisine that kept the Hussite warriors fit, turn towards **U dvou kocek**, a pub at Svatosova 310, which combines Slovak cuisine with Hussite-theme decor.

Castle Gardens

Although Tábor is relatively quiet, even at weekends, there are times when it seems that half of Prague, complete with babies in prams or buggies and picnics of varying sizes, gathers in the magnificent gardens and green parks of **Castle Konopiště**. The castle, whose grounds were laid out in the 13th century, has, like the country as a whole, had a turbulent history. Here, in 1423, in the midst of a war with the emperor's troops, the Hussites argued amongst themselves about disputed liturgical questions. In the course of the Thirty Years' War the Gothic castle was laid waste by the Swedes; it was later rebuilt in the baroque style. The Habsburg heir Archduke Franz Ferdinand – whose assassination in Sarajevo in 1914 was to precipitate the outbreak of World War I – erected a stately private palace in Konopiště, which he filled with an extravagant collection of art objects.

The large dining room, whose tapestries depict scenes from Cervantes' *Don Quixote*, is of particular interest. The smoking room, the library and

Above: the castle, where the Hussites argued over liturgical matters
Right: colonnades at Karlovy Vary, once the world's most cosmopolitan resort

the chapel on the second floor, and the countless hunting trophies in the corridors and stairways, testify to the extravagant lifestyle of the castle's master and guests. Only part of the gigantic castle park, with its aromatic rose gardens, ponds and wildlife pens, is open to the public. If you get thirsty, there is a tavern here, and another one not far from the car park.

Once you have had your fill of Konopiště, proceed along a small side road west into the romantic valley of **Sázava**, and then several kilometres north towards **Jilové u Prahy**, where a small street immediately leads off to the left, towards **Davle**. Crossing the Upper Vltava by means of a bridge that seems to groan with old age, you can, depending on the time you have remaining, either drive left into the Vltava Valley for a bit of spontaneous sightseeing, or take the right-hand road back to Prague.

3. KARLOVY VARY *(see map p56)*

Visit Karlovy Vary (Carlsbad) – the most famous of west Bohemia's lovely spas. If there's time you might also see the others: Františkový Lázně (Franzensbad), Mariánské Lázně (Marienbad) and Jáchymov.

Buses leave regularly for Karlovy Vary from Prague's Florenc station, starting at 8.45am. The journey takes about two hours and 15 minutes.

Easily reached by car, train, or, in the case of Karlovy Vary, plane, the spas of west Bohemia exude a demure charm and impart a sense of old imperial elegance. **Karlovy Vary/Carlsbad** has the longest tradition; it was here, according to the legend, that Emperor Charles IV discovered the healing spring by accident while on the trail of a magnificent stag during a hunting expedition from nearby Castle Loket. The imperial physician determined that the water had a therapeutic effect, whereupon the emperor, in 1349, founded a settlement which received its city charter in 1370.

At the end of the 18th century, Karlovy Vary became the most cosmopolitan resort in the world. Crowned heads and celebrated artists alike enthused about the health-giving waters. Peter the Great came here twice – ostensibly to discuss Russian advances in science and culture with the great philosopher

Leibniz – and it's documented that Goethe visited the place no fewer than 13 times. Nowhere else, he said, could provide 'a more comfortable and pleasant visit'. The list of other guests who stayed at the resort is impressive. It includes European financial magnates who liked to stay in the 'Sanatorium Imperial'; aristocrats, who tended to prefer the elegance of the Grand Hotel, which was owned by Johann Georg Pupp, a former baker. Karl Marx is said to have written several chapters of *Das Kapital* here, no doubt inspired by the presence of so many members of the exploiting classes.

Karlovy Vary has also been the venue of more immediate political manouevres. In 1819, for instance, just four years after the Congress of Vienna was supposed to have clinched peace across the continent, the Austrian chancellor, Prince Metternich, invited representatives of all friendly nations to a council here, whereupon he issued the Carlsbad Decrees. These, in effect, were a declaration of war upon all peacemaking efforts in Europe.

Arriving by Car

In those days the carriage trip to Karlovy Vary through the narrow Valley of Teplá was a dangerous expedition. Today the greatest threat is posed by the arcane structure of the local road system. *Don't* follow the signs to Mariánské Lázně or Prague, or you will be led into the modern, northern section of the town. There is virtually no parking there and it will prove almost impossible to drive back to the south. Rather aim for the south side of the town, and you might be lucky enough to find a parking space at the foot of Teplá, or on the embankment.

Once you have parked, begin the walking part of this itinerary on the left bank of the river. The most notable feature along here is a row of stately buildings which includes the ornate **Casino** and the enormous **Grand Hotel Pupp**. The main entrance to the old Grand Hotel – which has a beautiful lobby, a stylish tea room and a luxurious restaurant – is set somewhat to the rear of the corner of Teplá.

Behind the hotel is a funicular (Lanovka) station, from where you can ride up the 200-metre (656ft) slope to **Friendship Heights** (Výšina Přátelství). Here a well-appointed observation tower and restaurant makes a good stop-off.

Alternatively, if you would rather continue with your walk, a stroll through the valley along the **Old Meadow** (Stará louka) leads to the most expensive shopping street in the town. This is where you will come to the headquarters of the world-famous glass and crystal manufacturer **Moser**.

Left: the ornate Grand Hotel Pupp

On the opposite bank of the river – and now easily reached by any one of a number of pedestrian bridges – Viennese architects built the renowned **Hotel Kaiserbad** shortly before the turn of the 20th century. Next to the hotel is the **State Theatre**, dating back to 1886.

Your walk should now bring you to **Tržiště** (Market Square), where a row of old-fashioned wooden stalls and the **Vřídlo Colonnade**, built in 1975, obscure the beautiful **Church of Mary Magdalene**, which was designed by Kilián Ignáz Dientzenhofer.

Twelve Springs

The **Mill Fountain Colonnade**, complete with its pump room, is the central point of this spa town, and should have a salutory calming effect. Here visitors have the opportunity to sample the water of one of the 12 springs that have made the town famous. Unfortunately the bathing complex to the north of here isn't particularly worth a visit, and a better option is to turn left and walk to the **Russian Church** (Ruský kostel). Once you have put the steep ascent up **Park Street** (Sadová třída) behind you, the reward is a beautiful panoramic view out over the town.

Some 70,000 Visitors come to Karlovy Vary for water therapy each year, and the resort's statistics are quite breathtaking. The mineral springs, which produce some 3,000 litres (659 gallons) of water per minute, provide the most essential ingredient of the resort's therapies. Vřídlo, the most famous of the various springs found in Karlovy Vary, spouts 3 million litres (659,700 gallons) of water at 70°C (158°F) every day. Drinking cures constitute the most important aspect of spa therapies, especially for treating digestive complaints and chronic liver and gall-bladder diseases.

Of course Karlovy Vary is not exclusively for those suffering from ill health. Beyond the famous 12 springs, it also offers the benefits of its '13th spring' – the renowned Becherovka-brand bitters. You might well appreciate the powerful effects of these alcoholic brews, but they are of dubious medicinal value.

Films and Opera

Visitors also descend on Karlovy Vary to take advantage of its cultural events. For instance, the film festival that takes place every summer here is graded 'A' in the international rankings and has gained a reputation for screening the most interesting films coming out of Central and Eastern Europe. The town also supports its own symphony orchestra and stages two music festivals: one for young musicians in August and a Dvořák festival in the autumn.

Right: a Karlovy Vary resident, dressed for an occasion

4. PILSNER BEER IN PLZEŇ (PILSEN) *(see map p56)*

By car, drive some 90km (56 miles) for two hours on the E50 to Plzeň.

Buses leave regularly for the city of Plzeň from Prague's Florenc Station, commencing at 8.15am. The journey takes about an hour and a half.

The first account of Bohemia's beer-brewing tradition dates to 1082. The industry's capital is **Plzeň** (Pilsen), and its product, Plzeňský Prazdroj, is known throughout the world as Pilsner. The city has a romantic, medieval centre, interesting sights, and lots of gastronomic options to accompany the beer. Founded in 1290, the city was quick to attract private breweries. The **Brewing Museum** (Pivovarské muzeum, open Tues–Sun 10am–6pm), which surveys the history of brewing, is in a late-Gothic malt-house in **Veleslavínova**, near the central Republic Square (Náměstí Republiky).

Tour of the Brewery

To the east of the Old Town, **U Prazdroje** street leads to the **Prazdroj Brewery** (or Urquell Brewery), where Pilsner beer has been produced since

1842. Enter through the imposing gateway for a tour of the premises, a visit to the brewery pub and to join a group tour (daily, 12.30pm). Like other beers, Pilsner is brewed by fermenting a mixture of ground malt, water and hops with beer yeast fungi. Pilsner owes its flavour and strength to the soft, low-sodium water, and to hops from Žatec in west Bohemia. The malt, made of roasted grain, is prepared according to a traditional recipe. Pilsner's cellars, where the beer matures for two to three months, and which are kept at 1–2°C (34–36°F), are cut deep into the sandstone bedrock. .

By 1865, three-quarters of the beer produced in Plzeň was being exported. In 1900, the legendary 'beer train' began its daily run from Plzeň to Vienna; later, a similar train went to Bremen, from where Pilsner Urquell was shipped to America. Today the annual production of the Prazdroj brewery alone amounts to 1,300,000 hectolitres (about 29 million gallons).

The Pilsen Madonna

The city, the country's third-largest, has other attractions too. Turn back to the imposing **St Bartholomew Church** in Republic Square. Inside is the famed marble 'Pilsen Madonna'. Nearby, at 65 Perlová Street, a deceptively plain-looking abode is the last relic of old Plzeň. An immaculately preserved Renaissance home in its own right, it leads into an amazing underground complex of damp passages, cellars and wells spanning the old city centre. The tunnels are open daily except Mon 9am–4.30pm. The 1892 **Great Synagogue**, one of Europe's largest, is sadly in a state of disrepair.

Above: Plzeň beer brewer. **Right:** the sign of genuine Pilsner
Far Right: the Gothic Cathedral of St Barbara in Kutná Hora

excursions

5. KUTNÁ HORA *(see map p56)*

Take a day trip to a historic mining town whose highlights include a stunning Gothic cathedral, the oldest mint in the region and the amazing, if somewhat ghoulish, Bone Church.

To reach Kutná Hora by car, take Highway 12 eastwards from Prague in the direction of Kolín. Alternatively, trains for Kutná Hora leave at approximately hourly intervals from Prague's main railway station, commencing at 9.05am. In both cases, the journey takes about an hour.

Though you would never realise it from a preliminary exploration of the quiet, peaceful little streets of this medieval town, Kutná Hora once rivalled Prague as Bohemia's cosmopolitan centre of affluence and influence. As you wander through the lanes, however, you will soon become acquainted with the grand evidence that remains of Kutná Hora's past glory. The town was founded in the 9th century, but the history of Kutná Hora only really kicked off in the late 13th century, when its massive deposits of silver and copper began to be mined in earnest. It was not long before the town became Europe's most important source of silver. In all, Kutná Hora produced some 50,000 tons of the precious metal before the mines ran out in the 18th century.

Prague Groschen

The best place from which to embark on a tour of the town is the **Vlašský dvůr** (Italian Court), a fortified palace founded in the 13th century. The palace became the main storehouse for Kutná Hora's silver as well as the region's first mint. It was here that the famous Prague groschen were pressed; the groschen was for centuries Europe's most stable currency. The palace also served as the occasional residence of Bohemia's kings, who no doubt appreciated the presence of so much precious metal, and money.

Today the site houses a museum devoted to the mint. The royal quarters are also open for tours. Also worth a visit is the **Information Centre** (open daily; Apr–Sept: 9am–6pm, Oct–Mar: 10am–4pm) just off the building's courtyard, where maps of the town and in-depth guidebooks are available.

From the Information Centre, continue past the 14th-century **Archdean's Church of St James** – you can't miss this imposing landmark – and on, up Ruthardská and Barborská streets towards the massive **Hrádek** ('castle').

First built in the 11th century as an officers' barracks, the castle was purchased by a local entrepreneur and royal officer in 1490. The next owner, using profits from an illegal mine and smelting operation that he was running under the castle, transformed it into the sumptuous palace we see today. The castle's **Museum of Mining** (open daily; Apr–Oct only: 9am–5pm) conducts tours of the former mine, for which authentic medieval miners' costumes and lanterns are provided . Once you have recovered from this subterranean experience, you might wish to avail yourself of some refreshment at the homey **Restaurace Kometa** (Barborská 29), which serves a limited selection of Czech and international dishes.

Five Hundred Years to Build

You will doubtless by now have noticed the singular architecture of the **Cathedral of St Barbara** (open: Tues–Sun; Apr–Oct: 9am–4pm, Nov–Mar: 9–11.30am, 2–3.30pm) which, with its oddly fluted roof and abundant buttresses, looms over the town. This, the real fruit of Kutná

Hora's former wealth, was funded almost entirely by the miners.

Given Kutná Hora's dwindling fortunes – and indeed the entire region's turbulent history – it is perhaps not surprising that it took more than 500 years to complete work on the cathedral. (Construction began in 1388 and was not finished until 1905.) The cathedral serves as a textbook example of the development of Gothic architecture in Bohemia. Moreover, it is the place to see some remarkable late-Gothic frescoes, immaculately restored period furnishings and a collection of baroque sacred art.

For all the glorious features of the Cathedral of St Barbara however, it is not Kutná Hora's most memorable attraction. That accolade belongs to a weird type of ossuary known as the **Bone Church** (which also goes by the name of Kostnice, open daily; Apr–Aug: 8am–noon, 1–6pm; Sep–Mar: 8am–4pm), which is located a mile outside the town – take a cab or, directed by signs from the town's main square, enjoy the walk. Decidedly not for the squeamish, this church features an interior ornately decorated with eye-catching 'sculptures' – including chandeliers and coats of arms – all created from 40,000 human bones taken from a local graveyard.

The origins of this macabre exhibition date back to the 13th century, when an abbot returned from a pilgrimage to the Holy Land with a handful of soil, which he scattered in the church's graveyard. As successive generations of the faithful clamoured to be buried here, the cemetery became overcrowded. In the 16th century, the bones were gradually exhumed, presumably due to lack of space, and a half-blind monk devoted his life to arranging them.

Above: exhibits at the Bone Church are not for the squeamish

6. ČESKY RAJ *(see map p56)*

A day trip to Bohemia's most beautiful nature reserve, whose attractions include castles, recreation areas and sandstone 'cities'.

To drive to Český Raj, take highway E65 northeast of Prague to Turnov – about an hour's drive. Alternatively, buses leave regularly for Turnov from Prague's Florenc Station, from 8.15am. The journey by bus takes about an hour and 45 minutes. You can also take a train from the city's main station (Hlavní nádraží).

The name Český Raj translates as 'Czech Paradise', and this nature reserve certainly lives up to its reputation. A hiker's dream, it is criss-crossed with cool, shaded, well-maintained and marked paths that lead from mountain hotel to stunning outlook point, from ruined castle to restored chateau. The reserve is also a geologist's fantasy: in the spring you are bound to see any number of rock-hunters tramping through freshly ploughed fields in their quest for specimens of agate, jasper, amethyst and garnet.

Turnov itself offers little for the sightseer but, if you want maps and tourist information, it is a good idea to stop by the **Čechotour** office at 5.května Street No 61, near the station. To begin your hike, follow the signs to pick up the red-marked trail a short distance from the station. Leaving the town behind, the trail begins a gentle rise towards the sandstone landscape. Český Raj marks the beginning of the foothills that eventually become the Krkonoše mountains. The first major landmark is **Valdštejn Castle**, a 13th-century fortress that was used in turn by Hussite rebels as a base, by bandits as a hideout, and by Albrecht of Wallenstein as a summer house.

Chance Your Arm with a Crossbow

Crossing the footbridge, with its striking array of baroque statues, you will probably be struck by the fortress's small **chapel** and the lovely view of the valley below from the battlements. Wander through the complex and you will find an aviary full of birds of prey.

You should also be presented with the rare opportunity to test your marksmanship with a crossbow. Another 2km (1 mile) down the red-marked trail is **Hrubá skála** – an extensive sandstone 'city' formed over millions of years as the elements eroded the ancient sea bed. The trail affords stunning views of these formations from several angles, and signs explain their geological origins.

If you only have a day to devote to Český Raj, you ought to begin the 5-km (3-mile) walk back to Turnov at this point. But if you are fortunate enough to have more time, the area has sufficient cultural and natural wonders to fill several days of fine hiking and camping.

Right: the 13th-century Valdštejn Castle

Leisure Activities

SHOPPING

Even before the fall of the Iron Curtain, Prague was known as the shopping paradise of the Eastern bloc. Visitors on weekend trips from Poland and East Germany came to shop by day and have a wild time in bars and nightclubs by night. Many of today's small shops and well-planned department stores were established in the city centre prior to the momentous events of 1989.

Bohemian glass and tableware are known throughout the world for their high quality. These items can be bought relatively cheaply in Prague due to the advantageous rates of exchange, although prices have risen in recent years. Factories are barely able to keep up with the tremendous demand.

Traditional Bohemian glassware – such as the baroque goblet with its polished foot, or the fine, thin, many-sided beaker – was intricately engraved with elaborate ornaments that featured flowers, garlands or grotesqueries. Today's glass, influenced by Art Nouveau, is known for its imaginative shapes, surprising colours and metallic effects. Beyond its practical usage, modern glass has become an art medium.

Western tourists have a reputation for succumbing to shopping fever and buying everything that isn't nailed down. And for good reason: numerous items that have long sold for high prices in the West can still be had in Prague for bargain prices. Antique dealers, however, tend to be very aware of developments in the Western markets – and their prices are accordingly high.

Art galleries are undergoing a boom period. The works of artists who were excluded from the artists' associations until 1989, in particular, are exhibited and sold everywhere. Crafts shops, too, are doing good business. Authorised outlets offer woodcarvings from all over the Czech Republic. Handmade jewellery, traditional Czech puppets and painted scenes of Prague are sold on street stalls, most commonly on Charles Bridge (Karlův most) or Na příkopě.

Open-air markets have in recent years sprung up along the pedestrian zones on Republic Square (Náměstí Republiky) and on Wenceslas Square (Václavské náměstí), where you will find an array of souvenirs, and all sorts of knick-knacks.

You can also get English- and German-language books for reasonable prices in Prague. Since the state ceased to subsidise book publication, Czech publishers have been faced with the prospect of financial ruin, and have had to increase their prices considerably in an effort to survive. For Prague natives therefore, buying books is unprecedentedly expensive, but for the foreigner, even Czech books – including lots of beautifully published art volumes – remain quite a bargain.

Classical music aficionados will find they can get good records, discs and cassette tapes at bargain prices.

A typical gift to take home is Prague ham, although not many butchers offer this on a

Left: café on Mala Strana
Right: Kafka and castle souvenirs

regular basis. It's far easier to find a bottle of the herbal liqueur Becherovka or a drop of good *slivovice*, a sort of plum brandy. Also recommended are the predominantly fruity wines of Bohemia and Moravia.

Russian dolls, of all shapes and sizes, are popular souvenirs: you'll find everything from the traditional babushka to those that anachronistically portray the images of Soviet leaders. Traditional Czech painted eggs, the ubiquitous puppets and wooden toys make typical and attractive gifts.

Shops are generally open Monday to Friday 9am–6pm, Saturday until 1pm, closed Sunday, although many tourist-oriented shops stay open much later, especially in the summer.

Glass and Porcelain

You won't have to look far to find shops that sell Bohemian crystal. The three listed here are the places to buy top-quality wares.

Moser

Na Příkopě 12–Nové Město
The elegantly appointed flagship store; and
Old Town Square
Prague 1–Staré Město
The best, most expensive Czech glassware.

Erpet

Staroměstské nám. 27
Prague 1– Staré Město
Tel: 24 22 97 55
Daily 10am–8pm. A wide range of top-of-the-range market crystal.

Crystalex

Malé nám. 6
Prague 1–Staré Město
Tel: 24 22 84 59
www.crystalex.cz
The factory store of this leading Bohemian manufacturer.

Folk Art and Crafts

Ceská lidová remesla (Czech Traditional Handicrafts)
Karlova 26
Prague 1–Staré Město
Tel: 22 22 04 33
http://shop.czech-tradition.cz
A chain of stores specialising in local crafts, including wooden toys, hand-dyed fabric, ceramics, and beautifully painted eggs. The chain has seven other locations, all situated along the main tourist routes.

International Booksellers

The following three book stores enjoy a reputation for stocking predominantly English-language titles.

Anagram Books

Týn 4
Prague 1–Staré Město
Tel: 24 89 57 37
www.anagram.cz

Big Ben Bookshop

Malá Štupartská 5
Prague 1–Staré Město
Tel: 231 98 48

The Globe Bookstore and Coffeehouse

Pštrossova 7
Prague 1–Nové Mesto
Tel: 66 71 26 10
www.globel.cz

The new location of this classic expat book store is geared more towards an upwardly mobile local crowd. Readings by local and international authors are sometimes held in the café. Free Internet terminals.

Fashion

Though you will find few international-label bargains, young Czech designers offer high quality for surprisingly reasonable prices.

Nostalgie

Locations at Husova 8
Jakubská 8 and Jilská 22
Prague 1–Staré Město
Tel: 26 62 56 (Jilská store)
Romantic lines by Marie Fleischmannová.

Boutique Klára Nademlýnská

Dlouhá 7
Prague 1–Staré Město
Tel: 24 81 87 69
Klára Nademlýnská's fashionable hand-made items.

Mýrnyx týrnýx

Saská ulička
Prague 1–Malá Strana
Tel: 29 79 38
Daily 11am–7pm. Vintage retro.

Bim Bam Bum-Galerie Gambit

Husova 8
Prague 1–Staré Město
Mon–Fri 11am–7pm, weekends 1–7pm. Children's fashions in natural fibres.

Model

Václavské nám. 28
Prague 1–Nové Město
Tel: 24 21 68 05.
Also at Vodičkova 14
Open Mon–Fri 9am–7pm; Sat 10am–5pm. High-quality hats.

Music

Classical music fans can find fine bargains on Czech-label CDs. Also look out for recordings by local jazz musicians and experimental rock groups.

Supraphon

Jungmannova 20
Prague 1–Nové Město
Mon–Fri 9am–7pm, Sat 9am–1pm. The first place to look for that classical disc.

Popron

Jungmannova 30
Prague 1–Nové Město
Mon–Fri 9am–7.30pm, Sat 9am–7pm, Sun 10am–6pm. Music of all types. Large section of Czech rock, jazz and pop; strong classical department downstairs.

Bontonland

Václavské náměstí 1
Prague 1–Nové Mesto
Mon–Fri 9am–8pm, Sat 10am–8pm, Sun 10am–6pm. The largest selection of music in Prague, including the biggest local groups. Booths allow you to listen before you buy.

Food

Dum lahudek (House of Delicacies)

Malé nám. 3
Prague 1–Staré Město
Four floors of both national and imported speciality foods; good wine shop.

Fruits de France

Jindřišská
Prague 1–Nové Město
and Bělehradská
Prague 2.
Good for salad greens, fresh fruit and cheeses; ideal if you're self-catering.

Bakeshop Praha

V Kolkovně 2
Prague 1–Staré Město
Daily 7am–7pm. Excellent baked goods to take away or to eat on the premises of this little shop.

Left: browsing for antiques

EATING OUT

Czech cuisine incorporates the hearty styles of Bohemian, Slovakian and Moravian cooking. Yet, for all the diversity of these three influences, no Czech meal, it seems, is complete without dumplings, made either of potato or bread. The other national dishes are roast pork with cabbage, and goulash, although these are certainly not exclusive to the Czech Republic, as anyone familiar with German and Austrian culinary traditions knows. A well-rounded meal generally starts with soup; after the main course, dessert often consists of a sweet pancake or apple strudel, usually with plenty of whipped cream.

The ubiquitous dumplings notwithstanding – and as long as you are not trying to stick to any form of strict diet – you can eat well in Prague. The meat dishes, whether they consist of pork, goose, or duck, can be very good. Vegetables – apart from cabbage or potatoes – do seem to be in short supply in restaurants serving Czech fare, however, and salads, on the occasions when they do appear, are largely disappointing. Vegetarians usually have a hard time with Bohemian cuisine. But the times are changing, and

Prague restaurateurs have not been slow to perceive a demand and cater for it. Consequently, a number of vegetarian places can be found in the city, and the menus of other restaurants may well be adjusted accordingly. Visitors on a budget will also be pleased to see that restaurants all over the Old Town and Malá Strana offer tourists menus (inexpensive set dishes).

The city's **coffee houses** have long been regarded as a Prague tradition. It is only since 1989 that they have breathed anew the atmosphere traditionally associated with such cafés. The **Slavia** and those in the hotel **Evropa** and **Obecní dům** *(Municipal House, see Nightlife, page 74)* are particularly recommended. Coffee house menus tend to offer light meals and snacks; to drink, you can order virtually anything.

Stand-up snack bars, or *bufets*, are an alternative to restaurant dining for many Prague residents at breakfast and lunch. Open from 7am to 6pm, they're just the thing for a not-too-costly bite to eat – provided you aren't a vegetarian or counting calories. In addition, for food-on-the-hoof, many squares and streets have developed a true fast-food culture through hot-dog and waffle stands. And there are always burgers: McDonald's established a presence in Prague in 1989 and usually does brisk trade.

Prague's **taverns**, known as *pivnice,* are made for drinking beer. Statistics show that Prague citizens, on average, put away about 150 litres (40 gallons) of beer, or *pivo*, every year. Most of this tippling is not done at home, but in one of the taverns or beer halls.

Some of these 1,500 or more taverns can look back on several centuries of history. Such places are the focus of Prague's social and political life. Under the Communist regime, they were the only place where one could discuss ideas and wax philosophical more or less freely. Here people tell stories, complain, laugh – and drink. Patrons are a mixed bunch: students, intellectuals and workers mingle with one another and, these days, with foreign visitors. People sit pressed closely together at long wooden tables, and

Left: alfresco dining

conversations can quickly develop between tourists and locals.

Some famous historic taverns have attracted organised tourism. The deal at **U Fleků** (Křemencova 9, Prague 1, open daily 9am–11pm, tel: 29 89 59), one of the city's oldest and most popular pubs, is that the townspeople vanish in the afternoon to make way for the tourists. At these times, the polyglot waiters work like Trojans. The pub, which has seats for nearly 1,000 customers – inside (under a Gothic ceiling) and in its garden – serves 6,000 hectolitres (158,500 gallons) of its dark, home-brewed beer every year, while a cabaret and live music entertains patrons.

It's a similar story at **U Svatého Tomáše** (Letenská 12, Prague 1, open daily 11am–midnight, tel: 53 63 65), in the vaulted cellars of a former monastery brewery. The stories behind many of Prague's historic brewing inns are recounted in numerous traditional anecdotes. In 1843, for example, the carter Salzmann gave the tailor Pinkas a taste of Pilsner beer. The tailor found the brew so good that he opened a bar. As a result, Pilsner beer is still served in **U Pinkasů** (Jungmannovno náměstí 15, Prague 1, open daily 8am–11pm, tel: 24 22 29 65).

Another pub famous for its Pilsner beer is **U Zlatého tygra** (Husova 7, in the Old Town, open daily 3–11pm, tel: 24 22 90 20). This is the place to which President Havel brought Bill Clinton for a beer when he visited Prague as US President.

U Kalicha (Na bojišti 12, Prague 2, open 11am–11pm, tel: 29 07 01) was made famous by Jaroslav Hašek's novel *The Good Soldier Švejk*. It is packed with Švejk memorabilia and is always crowded.

Taverns that are less well-known to tourists and more authentically local include:
• **U Medvídků**, Na Perštýně 7, Prague 1 (tel: 24 22 09 30)
• **U Schnellů** Tomášská 12, Prague 1
• **U Černého vola**, Loretánské nám 1, Prague 1 (tel: 20 51 34 81).

Most of the following taverns serve basic, wholesome meals on the lines of roast beef or pork with sauerkraut and dumplings, goulash, and, occasionally, venison.

Bohemian Fare
U Medvídku
Na Perštýně 7
Prague 1–Staré Město
Traditional beer hall that serves big portions of well-made Bohemian specialities.

Novoměstske pivovary
Vodičkova
Prague 2–Nové Město
Busy micro-brewery that serves delicious Czech food in a winding labyrinth of rooms.

Pivnice Radegast
Celetná
Prague 1–Staré Město
Gothic beer hall featuring traditional fare at low prices. Excellent goulash.

Restaurace Pivovarský dum
Lipova 15
Prague 2–Nové Město
Tel: 96 21 66 66
Recently established micro-brewery that offers good Czech specialities along with its brew. Try the champagne or coffee beer.

Na Vysehrade
K Rotundě 2
Prague 2–Vyšehrad
Tel: 24 23 92 97
A fine place for refreshments in Vyšehrad. Large summer terrace.

U Kalicha
Na Bojišti 12–14
Prague 2
Tel: 29 07 01
Lots of old-time atmosphere at the pub where *The Good Soldier Švejk* made a date for 'six in the evening after the war'.

U sedmí Svábu
Jánský vršek 14
Prague 1–Malá Strana
Huge portions in a medieval atmosphere.

eating out

U Provaznice
Provaznická 3
Prague 1–Nové Město
Tel: 24 23 25 28
Old pub atmosphere; outstanding goulash.

Klub Architektu
Betlémské náměstí 5a
Prague 1–Staré Město
Tel: 24 40 12 14
Gothic cellar with a fine selection of updated classic Czech dishes and international fare.

Refined Dining

For elegant dining, the following are cheap by European standards:

Bellevue
Smetanovo nábřeži. 18
Prague 1–Staré Město
Tel: 22 22 14 38
Excellent food, romantic setting, fine view, near Charles Bridge. Jazz brunch on Sun.

Circle Line Brasserie
Malostranské náměstí 12
Prague 1–Malá Strana
Tel: 57 53 00 21
Continental delights in a cosy, sophisticated atmosphere. Impeccable service.

Hradcany Restaurant
Hotel Savoy, Keplerova 8
Prague 1–Hradčany
Tel: 24 30 24 30
Formal, elegant setting. Sushi buffet on Sun.

Parnas
Smetanovo nábřeží 2
Prague 1–Nové Město
Tel: 24 21 19 01
Continental cuisine, fine views.

Vojanuv dvur
U Lužickeho semináře 21
Prague 1–Malá Strana
Tel: 57 53 37 79
Well-appointed restaurant in the former home of the great thespian Eduard Vojan.

Palffy palác
Valdštejnská 14
Prague 1–Malá Strana
Tel: 57 32 05 70
Located in a former palace below the castle. The cuisine shows attention to detail without being fussy.

U Maltezských rytíru
Prokopská 10
Prague 1–Malá Strana
Tel: 53 63 57
Meat specialities and great apple strudel. When booking a table, try to reserve a place in the tiny basement area.

U Modré kachnicky
Nebovidská 6
Prague 1–Malá Strana
Tel. 57 32 03 08
Excellent game dishes – fallow deer haunch, roasted rabbit, venison – and elegant decor.

U Vladáre
Maltézské nám. 10
Prague 1–Malá Strana
Tel: 53 81 28
Two restaurants in one: a sophisticated *vinárna* (wine bar) on one side and a less formal *konírna* (former stables) on the other.

Vegetarian

Although the emphasis in Czech cooking is definitely on meat, vegetarians will find an increasing number of restaurants offering alternatives, usually in a relaxed atmosphere.

Bar Bar
Všehrdova 17
Prague 1
Tel: 57 32 03 08
Daily 11am–midnight. Crêpes and salads. Not exclusively vegetarian.

Country Life
Melantrichova 15 (entrance on Michalská)
Prague 1–Staré Město
Daily 9am–9.30pm (Fri –6pm). Eatery with vegetarian food to take away.

Lotos
Platnéřská 13
Prague 1–Staré Město
Tel: 232 23 90
Serene restaurant featuring fresh and healthy ingredients in a smoke-free environment.

Radost FX Cafe
Bělehradská 120
Prague 2
Tel: 24 25 47 76
Daily 11.30am–4am. Popular choice for good salads, soup and pasta. Usually crowded for weekend brunches.

U Govindy Vegetarian Club
Prague 1–Nové Město
Popular cafeteria-style Hare Krishna joint. A tearoom sells scrumptious baked goods.

International
More and more international restaurants are opening. The following are reliable bets.

Cicala
Žitná 43
Prague 2–Nové Město
Tel: 22 21 03 75
Great-value, family-run Italian. Try the antipasti buffet or the home-made tiramisu.

La Perle de Prague
Rašínovo nábřeží at Resslova Street
Prague 2–Nové Město
Tel: 21 98 41 60
Excellent and expensive French cuisine on the top of the Ginger and Fred building.

Pravda
Pařížská 17
Prague 1–Staré Město
Tel: 232 62 03
Hip, eclectic, cosmopolitan restaurant.

Red Hot and Blues
Jabuská 12
Prague 1
Tel: 231 46 39
Set in the old royal stables, and known for

Right: refined dining

its tasty Cajun and American specialities. Live jazz or blues in the evenings.

Don Giovanni
Karoliný Světlé 34
Prague 1–Staré Město
Tel: 22 22 20 60
Fresh seafood and top-of-the-line Italian food located just a stone's throw from the Charles Bridge.

King Solomon
Široká 8
Prague 1–Staré Město
Tel: 24 81 87 52
Kosher dishes such as gefilte fish, chicken soup and blue carp with prunes served in the heart of the Jewish Quarter.

Koto
Mostecká 20
Prague 1–Malá Strana
Tel: 53 14 60
Sushi establishment lovingly presided over by Mr Hachiro Tsuda from Kyoto.

Pasha
U lužického semináře 23
Prague 1–Malá Strana
Tel: 57 53 24 34
Middle Eastern cuisine, including a wide variety of appetisers and delectable desserts, served in a sumptuous setting.

NIGHTLIFE

As twilight descends, a romantic veil is drawn over Prague. Illuminated by old street-lights, the city invites long, leisurely strolls through its moonlit streets.

To start the evening, there are plenty of small bars and cafés for pre-dinner drinks. If you want to sample the herbal liqueur Becherovka, drop into one of the many bars on the west side of Charles Bridge, behind the archway in Lesser Town (Malá Strana).

For wine, beer, and other alcoholic drinks, as well as coffee, the city's stylish, comfortable coffee houses generally stay open until around 11pm. Recommended are the lovely Art Nouveau cafés in the **Hotel Evropa**, the **Hotel Paříž** and the Obecní dům (Municipal House), and, recently reopened on Národní třída, with a gorgeous view of the Vltava and Prague Castle, **Kavárna Slavia**. These venues frequently have live music in the evenings.

For dinner, try a *vinárna* (wine cellar) or one of the many restaurants that have recently opened. In the high season book ahead if you want to dine at a popular place.

When it comes to cultural activities, Prague is often cheaper than other capitals. Walk through the city in the early evening or

sometimes at lunchtime, and you are bound to hear the sounds of organs, violins and pianos emanate from churches, palaces and monasteries. The music played in historic buildings' ornate halls constitutes not only a concert, but a cultural experience. The **Convent of St Agnes'** concert hall or the Chapel of Mirrors in the Klementinum, for example, are worth a visit just for the settings.

Some of the city's 25-plus theatres stage productions specifically for foreign visitors: **Nová Scéna** (now called the Laterna Magika) and the **National Theatre** often mount foreign-language performances. Prague is the home of the English-language **Black Box** and the multinational **Misery Loves Company** troupes; a variety of mime and puppet shows transcend language; and there's the **Black-light Theatre**, whose main venue is now at the Nová Scéna (Laterna Magika). Most theatre performances begin at around 7pm. Book tickets in advance.

Prague is big on jazz. **Reduta** is the city's most famous jazz club, and there's also **Jazz Club U Staré paní**, **Agharta Jazz Centrum** and the tiny **U Malého Glena**. The English-language press, including *Culture in Prague*, have listings. Street posters also promote forthcoming theatre and concert events.

The late-night scene is not as developed as that of other European capitals, but it is catching up. The clubbing world is always in a state of flux: the venues listed here have either stood the test of time or have become very popular. See the English-language *Prague Post* newspaper for club listings.

Hotel discos tend to be tourist traps, and can be frequented by prostitutes looking for customers. There is usually a 'smart casual' dress code at these discos. The old night-clubs around Wenceslas Square, such as Hotel Ambassador's prominent **Alhambra Club**, now include striptease-type shows.

Casinos in the Wenceslas Square hotels are open to all but there is usually a dress code (no jeans or training shoes). These establishments tend to have an extensive array of cheap drinks. Most discos, clubs and casinos stay open until 5am.

Left: overlooking Wenceslas Square

Cafés

Blatouch
Vězeňská 4
Prague 1–Staré Město
Mon–Fri 11am–midnight, Sat 2pm–midnight, Sun 2–11pm. Trendy and smoky.

Cafe Evropa
Václavské náměstí 25
Prague 1–Nové Město
Daily 7am–midnight. Faded elegance. Great location for people-watching.

Cafe of Obecní dum
Náměstí Republiky
Prague 1–Nové Město
Daily 7.30am–11pm. Art Nouveau top to bottom.

The Globe
Pstrossova 6
Prague 1–Nové Mesto
Daily 10am–midnight. English-language bookstore with a café.

Kavárna Slavia
Smetanovo nábř. 2
Prague 1–Nové Město
(entrance on Národní třída)
Mon–Fri 8am–midnight, Sat, Sun 9am–midnight. This venerable café was once the haunt of Prague's intelligentsia.

St Nicholas Café
Tržíště 10–Malá Strana
Mon–Fri noon–1am, Sat, Sun 4pm–1am. Hip and laid-back.

Café Imperial
Na Poříčí 15
Prague 1–Nové Město
Daily 9am–1am. A gorgeous, ballroom-like atmosphere set to a 1920s jazz theme.

Ebel Coffee House
Týn 2
Prague 1–Staré Město
Open daily 9am–10pm. Quality coffee served just behind Old Town Square.

Káva Káva Káva
Národní 37
Prague 1–Nové Město
Mon–Fri 7am–9pm. Quiet courtyard café, delicious baked items and the city's best java.

Kavárna Rudolfinum
Alšovo nábřeží 12
Prague 1–Staré Město
Tues–Sun 10am–6pm. Big, elegant venue.

Café Louvre
Národní 20
Prague 1–Nové Město
Daily 8am–11pm. Café patronised by Kafka.

Clubs

Agharta Jazz Centrum
Krakovská 5
Prague 1–Nové Město
Tel: 22 21 12 75
Daily 5pm–midnight; the music starts at 9pm. Tiny venue, the best local jazz.

Delux
Václavské náměsti 4
Prague 1– Nové Město
(in Astra palác passage)
Daily 5pm–4am; live jazz 8–11pm, DJs 11pm–4am. Jazz and salsa dancing.

Jazz Club U Starí paní
Michalská 9
Prague 1–Staré Město
Tel: 26 72 67 to reserve seating
Daily 7pm–1am. Live jazz, starting at 9.

Reduta Jazz Club
Národní 20
Prague 1–Nové Město
Tel: 24 91 22 46 for table reservations
Daily 9pm–2am. Prague's top jazz club.

Palác Akropolis
Kubelíkova 27
Prague 3–Žižkov
Tel: 22 71 22 87
www.spinet.cz/akropolis
The best Czech and international music.

Roxy
Dlouhá třída 33
Prague 1–Staré Město
Tel: 24 82 63 90
Daily from 7.30pm. DJs, theatre or film.

Mecca
U průhonu 3
Prague 7–Holešovice
Daily 11am–5am. Hip restaurant and club.

Jazz Club Zelezná
Železná 16
Prague 1–Staré Město
Daily 4pm–11pm. Intimate Gothic cellar with good jazz. Get there early.

Karlovy lazne
Novotného lavka 1
Prague 1–Staré Město
Daily 7pm–5am. From trance to pop.

U Malého Glena
Karmelitská 23
Prague 1–Malá Strana
Daily 11am–2 am. Live jazz from 9pm.

Radost FX
Bělehradská 120
Prague 2
Daily 11am–5am. House music till morning. Popular with young movers and shakers.

Bars and Pubs
Baracnická rychta
Tržiště 23
Prague 1–Malá Strana
Daily noon–midnight. Cheap beer, solid pub fare; Austro-Hungarian empire ambience.

Bugsy's Bar
Kostečná 2
Prague 1–Staré Město
Daily 7pm–2am. Excellent cocktails.

Escape
Dušní 8
Prague 1–Staré Město
Daily 7pm–2am. Elegantly casual setting.

Jáma
V Jámě 7
Prague 1–Nové Město
Daily 11am–1am. Rock & roll, greasy food.

James Joyce
Liliová 10
Prague 1–Staré Město
Daily 10.30am–12.30am. A cosy, popular Irish pub with Czech, Irish, English beers.

O'Che's
Liliová 14
Prague 1–Staré Město
Daily 10am–midnight. A mix of Cuban *cantina* and Irish bar. Attracts foreigners.

Propaganda
Anny Letenské 18
Prague 2–Vinohrady
Mon–Sat 11.30am–midnight. This popular neighbourhood bar attracts a lively young Czech crowd.

Tretter's
V Kolkovně 3
Prague 1–Staré Město
Daily 7pm–3am. The connoisseur's choice for top-notch cocktails and service in a classy setting.

Gays and Lesbians
A Klub
Milíčova 32
Prague 3
Tel: 22 78 16 23
Daily 7pm–6am. Fri: women only; on other nights men admitted with female escort.

Riveria
Narodni 20
Prague 1
One of the trendiest gay bars.

U Strelce
Karolíny Svetlé 12
Prague 1
Daily 6pm–4am (Fri, Sat–6am). Gay, lesbian and straight. Cabaret.

Right: preparing for a traditional celebration

CALENDAR OF EVENTS

The calendar of Czech holidays was reconfigured after 1990. Though some traditional holidays remain unchanged, those associated with communist rule have been replaced.

January
Three Kings' Day (6th): trios dressed as the wise kings roam local pubs and sing folk songs in exchange for beer or money.

February
Masopust (Carnival), in the Žižkov district of Prague before Lent, features a procession. **St Matthew's Fair** (Matějská pout'), towards the end of the month, draws families with children to the Výstaviště.

March
On **Easter Monday** boys whip girls with beribboned willow switches (it's an ancient fertility ritual) and are given painted eggs. The **Days of European Film** festival (www.eurofilmfest.cz).

April
The **Prague Writers' Festival** draws world-class names (www.pwf.globalone.cz). On **Witches' Night** (Čarodějnice, 30th) crowds burn an effigy; all-night bonfire parties on Petřín Hill and Kampa Island.

May
May Day (1st) workers' holiday. Holidays mark the 1945 **Prague Uprising** (5th) and the end of **World War II** (8th). The **International Prague Spring Music Festival** begins on the 12th, the anniversary of Smetana's death, with a procession from his grave at Vyšehrad Cemetery.

June
Tanec Praha (www.tanecpha.cz) is an international dance festival.

July
Public holidays honour **SS Cyril and Methodius** (5th), and **Jan Hus** (6th). **International Karlovy Vary Film Festival** (www.iffkv.cz).

August
Anniversary of the 1968 invasion (20th).

September
Vintners' festivals (vinobraní) in Mělník and wine-growing regions of Moravia. **Prague Autumn Music Festival** (www.pragueautumn.cz).

October
The **Great Pardubice Steeplechase** (www.pardubice-racecourse.cz). The **Day of the Republic** (28th).

November
Velvet Revolution holiday (17th).

December
On the eve of **St Nicholas' Feast Day** (5th), costumed characters give fruit or sweets to children. At the start of **Christmas** (24–26th), churches host organ and choral concerts. **Midnight Mass** in St Vitus' Cathedral.

Practical Information

GETTING THERE

By Car

If you want to drive in the Czech Republic you will need a national driving licence, registration papers, international green card insurance, and a nationality sticker on your car. You must also be over 21 years old.

Speed limits are:
- 60km/h (38mph) in residential areas
- 110km/h (68mph) on motorways
- 90km/h (56mph) on country roads.

Be careful not to speed, as this is an offence punishable with on-the-spot fines. Drink-driving is also strictly forbidden.

If driving across one of the country's borders, be prepared for queues at crossings during the summer months. Unleaded petrol can be found at the majority of large petrol stations at prices comparable with the rest of mainland Europe.

By Train

There are direct trains to Prague from:
- Stuttgart (an 8-hour trip)
- Munich (8 hours)
- Frankfurt (10 hours)
- Berlin (6 hours)
- Hamburg (10 hours)
- Vienna (6 hours).

The main railway station in Prague is Hlavní nádraží (Wilsonova Station), which is close to the centre of the city and has a left-luggage office. The station's splendid Art Nouveau decor on the upper levels makes it a wonderful place for an initial experience of Prague.

By Plane

Ruzyně, Prague's only international airport, is situated about 15km (10 miles) from the city centre. It has recently been renovated and now provides all the usual facilities, including car rental and left-luggage offices. ČSA, the Czech Republic's national airline, operates a regular bus service to the Vltava terminal in Prague – the journey takes about 30 minutes.

Alternatively, there is a slower, cheaper, shuttle service. Although you will probably find rows of Belinda taxis lining up outside the terminal building, be warned that their prices are high.

Many of the world's major airlines now fly to Prague. The flight from London takes just under 2 hours.

By Bus

For those travelling on a budget, there are now a great many different bus tours to the Czech Republic, some of which are highly recommended. Check with coach companies in your country for the best deals. They can be very cheap and some also include hotel accommodation.

The main coach station is Florenc, where there is also a convenient metro stop for onward journeys straight to the city centre. For advance information ČSAD (national coach operators) have an English office at: 103 Wetheral Drive, Stanmore, Middlesex, HA7 2HH, tel: 020-8907 0962.

Left: new twists on an old idea
Right: at your service

TRAVEL ESSENTIALS

Visas

Citizens of countries that are members of the European Union require passports, but not visas, for stays of up to 90 days.

Citizens of the US need passports only for stays of up to 30 days.

Citizens of Canada, Australia and New Zealand need visas to enter the country.

Customs

Import: visitors are permitted to bring the following personal items into the country duty-free:

- 250 cigarettes or 50 cigars or 250g (9oz) of tobacco.
- 2 litres of wine, 5 litres of beer, 1 litre of spirits (to purchase tobacco and alcohol you must be over 18 years old).

You are allowed to bring unlimited amounts of foreign currency into the country.

Export: you may take gifts worth a total of 500 crowns out of the country but you must have a licence to export antiques (enquire when you make the purchase).

Animals: if you want to bring a pet dog or cat with you through customs, you must be prepared to show a certificate of inoculation that is between three days and three weeks old.

Electricity

Czech outlets are 220 Volts, and you need two-pin plugs.

Climate

The climate in the Czech Republic is typified by warm summers and lengthy, dry, cold winters. At the height of summer, in July and August, the temperatures can soar.

Tipping

In general, it is customary to round up the total when paying a bill in a beer hall or café. A 10 percent tip is customary in restaurants and for taxi drivers.

Currency and Credit Cards

Czech crowns (Koruna or Kč) circulate in denominations of 20, 50, 100, 200, 500, 1,000, 2,000 and 5,000-crown banknotes; the coins are for 1, 2, 5, 10, 20 and 50 crowns. There are also smaller denominations of 10, 20 and 50 hellers (100 hellers to the crown).

Eurocheques and the major credit cards are increasingly acceptable, but don't assume that you can use them everywhere. Always check first.

You can change currency and traveller's cheques in any of the city's larger hotels, as well as at exchange offices and banks. Exchange offices and travel agencies are open on weekdays until about 9pm; the central ones stay open late at weekends and at other times too during the summer months.

In October 1995 the Czech parliament voted to make Czech crowns convertible. This means that currency can be bought outside the Czech Republic and it is no longer illegal to bring it into the country.

GETTING ACQUAINTED

Politics

Czechoslovakia was divided into two quite separate republics on 1 January 1993. The Czech Republic is currently governed by a minority administration of the Social Democrats with the 'opposition agreement' of the right-wing Civic Democratic Party (ODS). The poet and dramatist Vaclac Havel is president of the republic, and Miloš Zeman is currently the prime minister.

Left: friendly smiles in a public park

Geography, Population, Religion

Prague, the ancient capital of the Czech Republic, is situated at latitude 50°8'N and longitude 14°32'E.

Prague has a population of approximately 1.3 million. About 10 percent of the republic's various industries are based in and around the city.

Since the Velvet Revolution, chapels and churches throughout the country have been undergoing major restoration work.

Although there are numerous Christian churches – both Roman Catholic and Protestant – in the Czech Republic, Prague, and Bohemia in general, are predominantly Protestant. Recently, particularly among the younger generation, non-Christian religions have begun to attract adherents.

HOURS AND HOLIDAYS

Business Hours

The majority of shops open at 9am and close at 6pm, but many smaller outlets, especially away from tourist centres, still close for an hour at midday. On Saturdays, most stores close at noon; the large department stores are an exception, staying open until 6pm. Many tourist-oriented shops in the centre of the city stay open until about 9pm during the summer season.

Banks are open Mon–Fri, 8am–5 or 6pm. Exchange offices remain open until at least 7pm every day; you might find some that don't close until 10pm.

Public Holidays

1 January New Year's Day
Easter Monday
1 May May Day/Labour Day
8 May End of World War II
5 July Day of the Slavonic Missionaries
6 July Anniversary of the death of Jan Hus
28 October Day of the Republic
17 November Day of Students' Struggle for Democracy
24–6 December Christmas Eve, Christmas Day and Boxing Day.

COMMUNICATION AND MEDIA

Print

Foreign newspapers can usually be found in hotels and kiosks, and in some of the major bookshops.

There are two English-language weekly papers in Prague: *The Prague Post*, which reports on news, business and cultural events as well as reviewing restaurants, clubs and shows, and the *Prague Business Journal.* The bi-monthly *Prague Tribune* focuses on business and executive lifestyles; *The New Presence* runs articles on political and social affairs translated from its Czech sister publication, *Nová Přítomnost.*

Several English-language literary publications are also based in Prague. These tend to publish the works of expatriate residents, international writers and artists, and translations of pieces by Czech writers. Look out for the monthly *Optimism*, the quarterlies *Trafica* and *Prague Review,* and the biannually published *Jejune: America Eats Its Young.*

You can pick up programmes of events, restaurant guides and general information brochures free of charge in tourist offices such as the PIS. The monthly English-language *Culture in Prague,* available at newsstands, lists all kinds of events and exhibitions.

Broadcasting

The two state-run television channels are ČT1 and ČT2. The latter broadcasts English-language European news both at midday and in the evening, as well as occasional movies and documentaries in English with Czech subtitles.

TV Nova and Prima are both privately owned stations that show popular Western serials dubbed into Czech, as well as local programmes.

BBC World Service can be picked up on frequency 101.1; it broadcasts the English-language Radio Prague in the afternoon and evening, with local news and features.

Post

Stamps *(známsky)* can usually be bought wherever postcards are sold. Ask about prices for stamps when you get there as the rates change with great frequency. You will find an information window inside most of these outlets.

Orange mailboxes can be seen everywhere. Post offices bear distinctive orange signs marked POŠTA. Larger ones are open Mon–Fri 8am–7pm, Sat 8am–12pm; smaller branches Mon–Fri 8am–1pm.

The General Post Office, located at Jindřišská 14, Prague 1 (tel: 21 13 11 11), just off Wenceslas Square, is open 24 hours a day, though with reduced services available at night.

Telephone, Telex and Fax

There are plenty of public telephones in Prague, but they don't always work. Some take 1, 2 and 5 crown coins, but most only

accept phone cards *(telefonní karta)*, which you can buy at newsagents and tobacconists, or from the main post office.

For the English-language operator, dial 1181. For long-distance calls, the most convenient option is to ring from your hotel – although hotels do have high commission charges – or from a post office. At the General Post Office in Jindřišská *(see above)* you can make calls 7am–11pm. The General Post Office also has a public fax service, as do some of the other larger post offices and major hotels.

Above: the badge of law

Internet Cafés

After a slow start, the Internet is finally taking off in the Czech Republic. There are numerous Internet cafés in Prague from which you can send e-mails or surf the Web.

Centrally located Internet cafés are:
• **The Globe**, Pštrossova 6, Prague 1 Nové Město, tel: 24 91 72 30. Open daily 9am–11pm.
• **Obecní dům**, Náměstí Republiky 5, Prague 1 Staré Město. Daily 8am–11pm. This café accepts e-mail for travellers at kavarna@ctg.cz.

EMERGENCIES

Emergency Numbers

First Aid	155
Fire	150
Police	158

Health Care

Medical emergency services are 24 hours a day. Emergency treatment is free but everything else must be paid for on-the-spot. Make sure you have medical insurance before you set off, and keep all receipts for treatment and medicine.

The **Diplomatic Health Centre** at Nemocnice Na Homolce, Roentgenova 2 (tel: 57 27 11 11) is specifically for foreign visitors. Alternatively, you can get medical treatment from English-language doctors at **Fakultní Poliklinika**, U nemocnice 2 (tel: 24 96 11 11), in the New Town. Remember to take your passport.

The **First Aid Centre** at Palackého 5 (tel: 24 94 77 17) is useful for minor problems. **Emergency Dental Service** can be obtained in Prague 1 (tel: 24 94 69 81).

Pharmacies *(lékárna)*, which are open for the duration of normal business hours, are also the places from which to obtain current information and addresses for emergency services. The most central of the city's pharmacies are at:
• Na Příkopě 7 (24 hours) and
• Wenceslas Square 64.

Breakdown Service

The official breakdown service (tel: 154) doesn't always stock spare parts for foreign cars. It's advisable to arrange for coverage from an automobile club before starting your journey. ADOS (tel: 67 31 07 13; open 24 hours) covers the Czech Republic. In Prague, try the office at Limuzská 12a (tel: 154).

Personal Safety

The Czech Republic has a relatively low crime rate. In recent years, however, petty crimes such as theft of and from cars and pickpocketing have increased considerably. Leave valuables in your hotel safe, and park your car in a supervised car park or garage. If you lose money or identification papers, apply to your consulate for assistance.

GETTING AROUND

Orientation

It's not difficult to find your way around Prague: the city's historic centre is compact and the most important sights can be reached on foot quite comfortably. The centre of the city (Praha 1) is divided into the historic quarters of Hradčany (the castle district), the Lesser Town (Malá Strana), the Old Town (Staré Město), and the New Town (Nové Město). The Lesser Town and Hradčany are situated on the left bank of the Vltava.

Linked to the Lesser Town by Charles Bridge (Karlův most), the picturesque streets of the Old Town have at their heart the busy Old Town Square (Staroměstské náměstí). The Jewish Quarter, known as Josefov or Židovské Město, is part of the Old Town.

The New Town, laid out in a semi-circle around the Old Town, has Wenceslas Square as its central axis. A futuristic metro line links the city centre with the suburbs, and provides an efficient and cheap means of transportation within the city centre. Public transport services also include old-fashioned trams, especially in the New Town. Ride on line 22 to get an idea of the city's layout.

Most of the city's best shops are located

around Wenceslas Square and in the adjacent street, Na Příkopě. Most of the best bars, restaurants and galleries are in the Old Town.

Public Transport

You can buy public-transport tickets at newspaper kiosks (look for the TABAK sign), and from automatic vending machines in the metro stations and at some tram stops. The tickets are valid for trams, buses and metros, and are inexpensive. Before entering the metro, and as soon as you board trams and buses, you must validate your ticket. A ticket is valid for any number of transfers within an hour-long period during the day, or for 90 minutes at night. Reduced-fare tickets are good only for 15 minutes of travel and you must validate a new ticket if you transfer between trams or buses; this doesn't apply for transfers between metro lines. You can buy single tickets, tourist tickets for designated periods, or transport passes, for one to five days. Children up to the age of six travel free; seven to 15-year-olds pay half.

Buses link the suburbs and the city centre, or service longer routes. For details about local or foreign connections, call Florenc Bus Station (tel: 24 21 02 21).

The **metro** is a quick and convenient way to get around the city. You can reach nearly all of Prague's major sights on the three lines, and it's easy enough to transfer from one to another. Underground stations are clearly marked with an 'M' sign. Services begin at 5am and end at midnight.

Above: the old-fashioned tram provides an excellent way to see the city

Trams are slow and old-fashioned, but offer a good way to see Prague (particularly Line 22, which runs past many highlights).

After midnight, **taxis** are the quickest way to get around. A few night trams and buses run at 40-minute intervals, but rates increase dramatically at night. There are lots of taxi stands in the city centre and in front of the large hotels, but these are best avoided. If you do flag down a taxi, try to negotiate a fare with the driver before setting off.

If phoning a taxi, AAA (tel: 33 11 33 11) and Profitaxi (tel: 61 31 41 51) both have English-speaking operators.

By Car

Safety belts must be worn on all car journeys – the country's traffic regulations are similar to those in most other European countries. Be warned however, that you should be particularly careful not to drink alcohol before driving, because the Czech Republic operates a zero-tolerance policy on this issue. You should also be sure that you have all the relevant papers, and that they are all in order, because cars are frequently stopped at random for document checks.

Parking regulations are complicated in the city centre – and the police and traffic wardens are extremely vigilant. At best you'll get a ticket, but you may well find your car has been clamped or towed away – both of which are time-consuming as well as expensive problems.

Car theft is also becoming increasingly common, so if you drive in Prague, the safest option is to leave your vehicle in a super-vised car park. There are several large ones in and around the city centre, all marked with large blue 'P' signs. These car parks are sometimes called 'Non-Stop'.

Car Rental

You can rent Hertz, Avis and Europcar vehicles from Europcar in Prague (credit cards accepted), providing that you can present a valid national driver's licence and are over 21. It's generally worth driving if you are using Prague as a base for touring the country, but not if you are planning to make only a few day trips.

For further information, contact:

Europcar
Parizska 28
Prague 1
Tel: 35 36 45 31

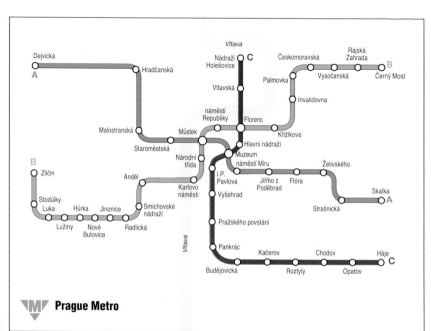

Prague Metro

practical information

FURTHER AFIELD

Domestic Flights

From Prague, the city of Ostrava is the only destination within the Czech Republic that is accessible by aeroplane. The national airline, ČSA (V celnici 5, Prague 1, tel: 20 10 41 11), can give you information about other connections.

By Train or Bus

The entire country is accessible by train and bus, and fares are relatively inexpensive. Fare and scheduling information for trains can be obtained from the main Hlavní nádraží railway station *(see Getting There, page 79)*. There is usually a clerk who speaks English at the main railway station's information office, which you will find on the mezzanine level.

You can buy tickets from the station from which you are due to depart; from Čedok, Na Příkopě 18 (tel: 24 19 76 43), or from a tour operator (such as Martin Tour: *see under Boat Trips below*). An excellent online train timetable, which has listings for domestic and international connections, can be found at http://idos.datis.cdrail.cz

You can purchase bus tickets and get information about connections – both within the Czech Republic and to sundry foreign destinations – at the Florenc bus terminal (tel: 24 21 02 21). Detailed information about connections can also be found online at http://timetable.svt.cz/cgi-bin/bus.pl/uk

Boat Trips

During peak season (1 May–15 Oct) there are popular sightseeing tours along the Vltava River. For details of this pleasant way to get a different view of the city, enquire at one of the PIS offices, or pick up a leaflet from one of the booths scattered around the city centre.

Martin Tour (Štěpánská 61, tel: 0603 459 954 or 24 21 24 73) runs various tours ranging in duration from 1½ to 3 hours, plus a 5-hour trip to Karlštejn Castle. The longer trips usually include lunch in the ticket price.

Right: a traditional form of transport

ACCOMMODATION

Hotels and Private Rooms

Although the cost of living in Prague is generally considered to be low when it comes to items such as food and drinks, accommodation can be quite expensive, even by Western standards. Moreover, reserving a hotel room in the city during the peak season can be problematic. A lot of hotels have fixed contracts with foreign travel agencies, which means that a reservation for a single traveller can be accepted only at very short notice. The best option might be to book through an agency. Increasing numbers of tour operators in Britain now specialise in Prague holidays.

The following are all recommended:

Cedok Tours
49 Southwark Street
London SE1 1RU
Tel: 020 7378 6009

Regent Holidays Ltd
15 John Street
Bristol BS1 2HR
Tel: 0117 9211 711

Time Off
Chester Close
Chester Street
London SW1X 7BQ
Tel: 020 7235 8070

When arriving in Prague, especially at the railway station, you might be accosted by people offering accommodation in private rooms or flats, and they may show you a photograph of the room. They are generally legitimate, and this can be an inexpensive alternative in a city with very high hotel – and occupancy – rates. But be aware that the lodging could be in the outer reaches of Prague or inconveniently located for public transport: you should ask to see the location on a map. The following organisations in England have details about private renting:

The Czechbook
52 St John's Park
London SE3 7JP
Tel: 020 8853 1168

Czechdays
89 Valence Road
Lewes
Sussex
BN7 1SJ
Tel: 01273 474 738

The following is a small selection of hotels.

Expensive
Doubles around 9,500Kč per night:

Hotel Inter-Continental
Namesti Curieovch 43
Prague 1– Staré Město
Tel: 24 88 11 11
http://www.interconti.com/prague
Riverbank location, with a stunning view of the castle.

Diplomat
Evropská 15
Prague 6
Tel: 24 39 42 15
One of the best business hotels in the city.

Dům U Červeného lva
Nerudova 14
Prague 1–Malá Strana
Tel: 53 72 39
Immaculate hotel five mins from the castle.

Hoffmeister
Pod Brudkou 7
Prague 1–Malá Strana
Tel: 51 01 71 00
One of the city's most stylish small hotels.

Hotel Palace
Panská 12
Prague 1–Nové Město
Tel: 24 09 31 11
http://www.hotel-palace.cz/
Restored Art Nouveau by Wenceslas Square.

Hotel Paríz
U Obecního domu 1
Prague 1–Staré Město
Tel: 22 19 51 95
www.hotel-pariz.cz
Art Nouveau elegance.

Savoy Hotel
Keplerova 6
Prague 6–Pohořelec
Tel: 24 30 24 30
www.hotel-savoy.com
Elegant 19th-century affair near the castle.

Moderate
Doubles around 6,500Kč per night:

Best Western City Hotel Morán
Na Moráni 15
Prague 2–Nové Město
Tel: 24 91 52 08
www.bestwestern.com/reservations/eu/cz/main.html
Great location near river and Charles Square.

Above: Prague is full of luxurious, old-world hotels

Hotel U Staré pani
Michalská 9
Prague 1–Stare Město
Tel: 24 22 80 90
A cosy hotel above one of Prague's best jazz clubs. Soundproof.

Kampa
Všehrdova 16
Prague 1–Malá Strana
Tel: 57 32 05 08
Hidden away in a quiet residential street.

Opera
Těšnov 13
Prague 1–Nové Město
Tel: 231 14 77
A recently refurbished old dame.

Hotel Adria
Václavské nám. 26
Prague 1–Nové Město
Tel: 21 08 12 93
www.hoteladria.cz
Amid the bustle of Wenceslas Square.

U trí pstrosu (Three Ostriches)
Dražického nám. 12
Prague 1–Malá Strana
Tel: 57 53 24 10
www.utripstrosu.cz
Situated in the shadow of the Charles Bridge.

Budget
Doubles around 3,500Kč per night:

Hotel Axa
Na Poříčí 40
Prague 1–Nové Město
Tel: 24 81 25 80
www.vol.cz/axa
Located in the New Town near the Florenc bus terminal.

Balkan
Svornisti 28
Prague 5
Tel: 57 32 71 80
Quiet, simple rooms, near Malá Strana.

Hotel pod vezi
Mostecká 5
Prague 1–Malá Strana
Tel: 57 53 20 41
A tiny, intimate affair just steps from the Charles Bridge.

Hotel Central
Rybná 8
Prague 1-Staré Město
Tel: 24 81 20 41
Located on a relatively quiet thoroughfare in the Old Town.

Hotel Cloister Inn
Bartolomějská 9
Prague 1–Staré Město
Tel: 232 77 00
www.cloister.inn.cz
Located on a quiet street in the Old Town, it also operates the lower-priced Unitas Pension *(see below)*.

Hotel Unitour
Senovážné náměsií 21
Prague 1–Staré Město
Tel: 24 10 25 36
An unbelievable find in the Old Town.

Pensions
Pension Dientzenhofer
Nosticova 2
Prague 1–Malá Strana
Tel: 57 31 13 19
The 16th-century birthplace of the baroque architect Kilián Ignáz Dientzenhofer, located above the romantic Devil's Stream, and just a stone's throw from Charles Bridge. Around 3,200Kč per night.

Unitas Pension
Bartolomějská 9
Prague 1–Staré Město
Tel: 232 77 00
www.cloister.inn.cz
Basic rooms in a former prison – you can request the 'cell' in which Václav Havel stayed. Rooms at the connected inn are more expensive.

Penzion Sprint
Cukrovarnická 64
Prague 6
Tel: 312 33 38
Basic economy rooms conveniently located just 20 minutes from the airport.

Pension U Raka
Cernínská 10
Prague 1–Hradčany
Tel: 20 51 11 00
A private guest house just behind the Loreto church.

Youth Hostels
Prague has a good selection of youth hostels, which are particularly recommended for travellers on a budget.

Travellers' Hostels
Dlouhá 33
Prague 1–Staré Město
Tel: 24 82 66 64
http://www.terminal.cz/~hostel
This chain of hostels has half a dozen centrally located outlets, with prices up to US$18 per person. The main branch, at Dlouhá 33, is open to travellers throughout the year; other branches are open during the summer season only.

Hostel Unitour
Senovážné námesti 21
Prague 1–Staré Město
Tel: 24 10 25 36
Quality rooms near the main train station; not to be confused with the hotel upstairs.

Domov Mladeže
Dykova 20
Prague 2
Tel: 22 51 52 24
A peaceful, clean hostel in a quiet residential district.

Welcome Hostels
The Welcome Hostels have several locations scattered throughout Prague. For information call the office (tel: 24 32 02 02).

CULTURE

Museums
National Museum
Václavské náměstí 68
Prague 1
Tel: 24 49 71 11
Daily except Tues, 9am–5pm.
Anthropology, archaeology, natural history.

Antonín Dvořák Museum
Ke Karlovu 20
Prague 2
Tel: 24 92 33 63
Daily except Mon, 10am–5pm.

Mucha Museum (Muchovo Muzeum)
Kavnický palác
Panska 7
Prague 1–Nové Město
Tel: 24 23 33 55
Daily 10am–6pm.
All about Art Nouveau doyen Alfons Mucha.

Náprstkovo Museum
Betlémské náměstí 1
Prague 1
Tel: 22 22 14 16
Daily except Mon, 10am–6pm.
Ethnographic collections from Asia, Africa and America.

National Technical Museum
Kostelní 42
Prague 7
Tel: 20 39 91 11
Daily except Mon 9am–5pm.
Exhibits on transport and astronomy.

Prague Municipal Gallery (Galerie Hl. Mesto Prahy)
House at the Golden Ring
Týnska 6
Prague 1–Staré Město
Tel: 24 82 70 22
Daily except Mon 10am–6pm.
Permanent collection of 20th-century Czech art, with galleries devoted to the leading contemporary artists.

**Museum of Decorative Arts
(Umeleckoprumyslove Muzeum)**
17. listopadu 2
Prague 1–Staré Město
Tel: 51 09 31 11
Daily except Mon, 10am–6pm.
Extensive collection of jewellery, furniture
and applied arts.

Smetana Museum
Novotného lávka 1
Prague 1
Tel: 24 22 90 75
Daily except Tues, 10am–5pm.

State Jewish Museum
Jáchymova 3
Prague 1
Tel: 24 81 00 99
Daily except Sat, holy days, 9.30am–5pm.

Strahov Monastery (Strahovský kláster)
Strahovské nádvoří 132
Prague 1 (Hradčany)
Tel: 24 51 11 37
Daily except Mon, 9am–5pm.

The **National Gallery** incorporates:
Sternberg Palace
Hradcanské námestí
Prague 1
Tel: 20 51 46 34
Daily except Mon, 10am–6pm.
European Old Masters.

St George's Monastery
Jirské nám. Hradčany
Prague 1 (Hradčany)
Tel: 57 53 16 44
Daily except Mon, 10am–6pm.
Czech Gothic, Renaissance and baroque art.

Veletrzni Palac
Dukelských hrdinů 47
Prague 7
Tel: 24 30 11 11
Daily except Mon, 10am–6pm (Thur –9pm).
19th-century, modern and contemporary art
in a gem of constructivist architecture.

Right: Dürer's *Festival of the Rosary*

Theatre
Prague has a lively theatre scene, as befits
one of Europe's great cities. Although
Czech-language plays may be beyond most
visitors, there is a range of other possibil-
ities that can be enjoyed. For dates and
times of performances contact the local
tourist office. Major theatres include the
following:

Estates Theatre (Stavoske divadlo)
Ovocný trh 6
Prague 1
Tel: 24 21 50 01

State Opera House (Statni opera)
Wilsonova 4
Prague 1
Tel: 96 11 71 11
This is the place to come to enjoy the best
in classical music.

Národní divadlo (National Theatre)
Národní třída 2
Prague 1
Tel: 24 91 34 37

National Marionette Theatre
Žatecká 1
Prague 1
Tel: 232 34 29
Marionette shows.

Nová Scena (Laterna Magika)
Národní třída 4
Prague 1
Tel: 24 91 41 29

Divadlo Ta Fantastika
Karlova 8
Palác Unitaria
Prague 1–Staré Město
Tel: 22 22 13 66
Black-light Theatre. (You can also see Black-light Theatre productions at Černé Divadlo Viřiho Srnce.)

Divadlo v Celetne
Celetná 17
Prague 1–Staré Město
Tel: 232 68 43
The English-language Black Box and Misery Loves Company theatre troupes share this venue with Czech companies.

Divadlo Spejbla a Hurvinka
Dejvická 38
Prague 6
Tel: 24 31 67 84
Puppet theatre in a city with an established tradition of this fascinating art form.

USEFUL ADDRESSES

Embassies and Consulates

United Kingdom
Thunovská 14
Prague 1
Tel: 57 53 02 78

USA
Tržiště 15
Prague 1
Tel: 57 53 06 63

Airlines
The leading airlines in Prague include:
Air Canada
Ruzyně Airport
Prague 6
Tel: 24 85 47 30

Air France
Václavské náměstí 10
Prague 1
Tel: 24 22 71 64

British Airways
Staroměstské nám. 10
Prague 1
Tel: 22 11 44 44

Czech Airlines (CSA)
Revoluční 1, Prague 1
Tel: 20 11 11 11

Delta Airlines
Pařížská 11
Prague
Tel: 24 94 67 33

KLM
Václavské náměstí 3
Prague.
Tel: 33 09 09 33

Lufthansa
Na Příkopě 24
Prague 1
Tel: 20 11 44 56

Above: the Municipal House illuminated at night

practical information

Religious Services
Anglican
St Clement's Church
Klimentská 5
Prague 1
Tel: 688 85 75
Service in English, Sun, 11am.

Catholic
Church of St Thomas
Josefská 8
Prague 1
Tel: 53 02 18
Sunday Mass, 11am in St Barbara Chapel.

Jewish
Old-New Synagogue
Maiselova
Prague 1
Services in Hebrew on Fri at sundown and Sat at 9am.

LANGUAGE

Pronunciation
Extended vowels are: á, é, í, ó, ů or ú, ý.
    Consonant sounds include:
    c as in tsar;
    ch as in the Scottish 'loch';
    j as in yes;
    č as ch;
    ň as n'ye;
    ř rolled with a gentle sh sound;
    š as sh.

Useful Words

ano	yes
ne	no
prosím	please
děkuji	thank you
dobrý den	good day
na shledanou	goodbye
promiňte	excuse me
kolik to stojí?	what's the price?
jedna	one
dva	two
jak daleko	how far?
dobrý	good
špatný	bad
levný	cheap
drahý	expensive
otevřeno	open
zavřeno	closed
mluvíte anglicky?	do you speak English?
nerozumím	I don't understand
nemluvím česky	I don't speak Czech
pivnice	beer hall
vinárna	wine bar
kavárna	coffee house

FURTHER READING

Reference
Insight Guide: Prague, Apa Publications. The most comprehensive title about the city, with stunning photographs, fascinating features and updated travel tips.

Insight Guide: Czech & Slovak Republics, Apa Publications. A combination of detailed and insightful reporting, with a photo-journalistic style of illustration.

Insight Compact Guide: Prague, Apa Publications. Essential itineraries and points of interest in and around the historic city, sumptuously illustrated with photographs.

We the People: The Revolution of 1989 by Timothy Garton-Ash, Granta. An authoritative account of the Velvet Revolution.

Fiction
The Good Soldier Svejk by Jaroslav Hašek, Penguin. Beloved Czech novel – the literary equivalent of Smetana's opera *Libuše*.

The Trial and **The Castle** by Franz Kafka, Penguin. Two of the most influential and prophetic novels of the 20th century. Also see the same writer's **Metamorphosis**.

The Unbearable Lightness of Being by Milan Kundera, Penguin. Celebrated tale of existential angst.

Tales of the Little Quarter by Jan Neruda, CEU Press. Turn of the 20th-century life in the Malá Strana

The Poetry of Jaroslav Seifert, Catbird Press. Collection of works by the Nobel Prize-winning writer.

INSIGHT
Pocket Guides

Insight Pocket Guides pioneered a new approach to guidebooks, introducing the concept of the authors as "local hosts" who would provide readers with personal recommendations, just as they would give honest advice to a friend who came to stay. They also included a full-size pull-out map. Now, to cope with the needs of the 21st century, new editions in this growing series are being given a new look to make them more practical to use, and restaurant and hotel listings have been greatly expanded.

☀ INSIGHT GUIDES

The world's largest collection of visual travel guides

Now in association with

ACKNOWLEDGEMENTS

Photography	
10	**Archives for Art & History**
11	**AKG London**
67, 73, 83	**Bodo Bondzio**
12T/B, 14T/B, 28T, 36, 37, 39, 43, 46B, 60, *61, 63, 77, 80, 85, 86, 90*	**Hansjörg Künzel & Alfred Horn**
57	**Jan Sagl**
58	**Jaruslav Kubec**
6T, 41, 62	**D Siegler**
7T, 13, 15, 16, 30, 34, 46, 59, 62, 70	**Bildagentur Jurgens**
23B, 24T, 26T	**K Vlcek**
74	**KU Müller**
38, 47, 48B, 49, 50, 51T, 53T/B, 64, 65, 68	**Jan Macuch**
5, 6B, 8/9, 21, 24, 25, 29, 30, 32, 40, 42, *45, 55, 56, 82*	**Mark Read**
1, 2/3, 8, 20, 31, 35, 44, 45, 52, 54, 66, 78	**Glyn Genin/APA**
Front Cover	**Pictures Colour Library**
Back Cover	**Mark Read/APA**
Design	**Carlotta Junger**
Cartography	**Maria Donnelly**

© APA Publications GmbH & Co. Verlag KG Singapore Branch, Singapore

INDEX